MERCHANT
TAYLORS'
SCHOOLS

MERCHANT TAYLORS' GIRLS' SCHOOL

M.T.G.S.

Ex Libris

CONCORDIA PARVE RES CRESCUNT

CONVICTS

CONVICTS

Transportation & Australia

MICHAEL BOGLE

Published by the Historic Houses Trust of New South Wales
The Mint, 10 Macquarie Street, Sydney NSW 2000, Australia
www.hht.net.au
First published 1999
Revised edition © 2008 Historic Houses Trust of New South Wales

This book was originally published in conjunction with the exhibition
Convicts [1999] at the Greenway Gallery, Hyde Park Barracks Museum,
Queens Square, Macquarie Street, Sydney, telephone 02 8239 2311.

Edited by Sandra Symons
Designed by Bruce Smythe
Pre-press by Spitting Image, Sydney
Printed by Imago Productions, Singapore

National Library of Australia Cataloguing-in-Publication entry:
    Bogle, Michael.
    Convicts: transportation & Australia / Michael Bogle.
    Rev. ed.
    ISBN 9781876991302 (pbk.)
    Convicts – Australia – History.
    Australia – History – 1788–1851.
    994.02

Cover: *Portrait of Chas [Charles] Rosetta*, part of *Tasmanian Views, Edward
Searle's Album of Photographs of Australia, Antarctica and the Pacific, 1911–1915*,
part of *EW Searle Collection of Photographs*, National Library of Australia

Title page: Augustus Earle, *A Government Jail Gang, Sydney N.S.Wales*
(detail), 1830, engraving from *Views in NSW and Van Diemen's Land*,
Mitchell Library, State Library of New South Wales

Back cover quote: Alexander Solzhenitsyn, *The Gulag Archipelago*,
Vols V–VII, Harper & Row, New York, 1974–78, p.335

CONTENTS

FOREWORD

This fascinating book has an importance beyond the guide which it offers to the exhibition on convicts at the Hyde Park Barracks Museum. It puts Australia's historical experience with convicts into the context of a dark story of exile and human suffering which reaches back, in recorded history, at least to ancient Egypt. It brings home to us, who have become sadly accustomed to the visual images of concentration camps and forced labour camps, how our modern Australian story began in circumstances not very different.

The Australian colonies would almost certainly never have been settled had the American Revolution not presented the British prison authorities with an obligation to find urgently an alternative place to dump the human cargo convicted by the British courts. At first, those authorities tried to send their convicts to the ports of the newly independent United States. Perhaps they thought the settlers would overlook the revolution and accept the prisoners as they had done in the past. When they turned the ships away, it became necessary to establish the penal settlement at Botany Bay, far away. In this sense, Australians are also children of the American Revolution.

Over 80 years following 1788, more than 160,000 souls were transported from the United Kingdom to the Australian colonies. They thereby escaped the public 'dance of death' which entertained the crowds at Tyburn or at

Newgate. But their fate was usually almost as dreadful. They were set to work building roads and public buildings; making tiles and bricks; sewing clothes and fashioning shoes. In the way of those times, the position of women was especially hard. Hunger, in those primitive days, was their constant companion. The first convict hanged in the penal colony at Sydney Cove met his fate in 1789 upon his conviction for raiding the precious food reserves. Those in charge were, if anything, even more strict and brutal in their dealings with the troops who stood guard over the convicts. A year later six Royal Marines were hanged for a like offence.

It is difficult for Australians today to recreate in their imagination the circumstances of the convicts and their guards in the settlements scattered around the coast of the newly acquired Australian continent and in Norfolk Island (where the most recalcitrant offenders were sent). The last convicts kept in the Hyde Park Barracks in Sydney marched out to the sight of St James Church in 1848, soon after the abandonment of transportation to the New South Wales colony in 1840. Yet the Barracks continue to this day to yield bones left over from their meagre meals. And if we close our eyes we can hear a symphony of sounds from those years: the screams that accompanied the brutal floggings administered as punishment, even for trivial wrongs; the tapping of unskilled artisans as they made shoes and brooms for the market; the sad lament of human beings with little prospect of returning to loved ones at Home, cursing the lack of food, companionship and affection.

It is really remarkable that Australians ever overcame this most unpromising start to their modern history. Yet in a remarkably short interval the free settlers, supplemented by convicts given tickets of leave and conditional release, began to build a civil society in Australia. Not everything in the story that followed was admirable. Although the penal administrators quickly engaged Aboriginals to track down escaped convicts, the convicts themselves, together with their descendants, soon set about heaping injustices on Aboriginal society which their own experiences ought to have made them determined to avoid.

The striking message to emerge from the tale of the convicts in Australia is how quickly the society set up to receive them turned to assert itself against the mother country and to demand an end of convict transportation.

When the British politicians and administrators (including, surprisingly, William Gladstone in an early manifestation) sought to insist on the revival of transportation, the Anti-Transportation League convened meetings in the colonies affected. Those meetings made it clear that, if pressed too hard, Australians would 'imitate the example of their brethren of the United States'. The British backed off. The last convict to arrive in Australia set foot in the Swan River colony in Western Australia in 1868. The 80-year experiment in penology and colonisation was over.

What is the legacy of the convicts? Is it a certain rebelliousness and distrust of authority and pretension? Is it Australia's often boasted claims to egalitarianism? Is it a certain roughness of our national character that makes us seem more at ease in a sports stadium than in a museum or in a concert hall? Is it a lingering fear that unless a firm hand insists on 'law and order', our genetic imprint will lead us back to the intolerable crimes that brought to Australia so many of the first arrivals who set the pattern of the waves of adventurers and refugees that followed?

The metaphor of the convicts is burned deeply into the Australian psyche. Most of the images of that time are, as this book reveals, cruel, painful and unyielding. Yet from that unpromising start a nation was fashioned. Its people were, within 50 years, showing their metal and demanding their rights. It was out of that determination that our Commonwealth was built. As we celebrate its centenary we must hope that, in its second century, we reacquaint ourselves with the painful early days. And dedicate our nation to upholding human rights and human dignity at home and abroad. If that is done, the spirits of the convicts and the guards who were shackled with them in fate will find peace. Out of suffering, justice. Out of cruelty, reconciliation. Out of indignities, human rights.

– THE HON JUSTICE MICHAEL KIRBY, AC CMG

High Court of Australia, Canberra

1 October 1999

PREFACE

This publication supplements the exhibition on convicts at the Hyde Park Barracks Museum [1999] by providing research and source material for the interpretation presented in the displays. Many people have played an important role in the development of this exhibition. Gary Crockett, former Assistant Curator; Samantha Fabry, Assistant Curator; Inara Walden, Assistant Curator; Myffanwy Sharpe, Researcher; Beverley Earnshaw, Historian; Jennifer Winlaw, Historian; Michael Trudgeon, Exhibition Designer; Richard Taylor, Exhibition Project Manager; and Caroline Mackaness, Exhibitions Coordinator have provided constant advice, research assistance and much-needed dialogue in developing the concepts we present to the public. The contribution of Beverley Earnshaw has been especially critical in locating material, and understanding and interpreting the convict period. The seminal insights of Peter Emmett's reinterpretation of the Hyde Park Convict Barracks for its 1991 reopening were invaluable. We also owe a debt of gratitude to our many other contributors whose names appear on the acknowledgments page.

– MICHAEL BOGLE

... these expelled felons created communities, cities, institutions and art that mirrored their unique experiences. Despite their dwindling population numbers among the free colonial settlers in Australia, convict lives dominated the political and cultural landscape of the colony.

INTRODUCTION

Flight from a European or Asian destiny traditionally led to freedom; Australia began its European history with a voyage into bondage. But the nation is not alone with its convict past. Criminals and political prisoners provided much of the vanguard for the 18th and 19th century European colonisation of Oceania, Asia and South America. In far-flung colonies, convict men and women were subjected to harsh physical and social conditions well beyond their experience and often exceeding their endurance. Convict transportation and penal settlements were worldwide phenomena.

Convicts built harbours, fortifications, theatres, courthouses, schools, churches, temples, governors' palaces, orphanages and even their own places of confinement. As time passed, these expelled felons created communities, cities, institutions and art that mirrored their unique experiences. Despite their dwindling population numbers among the free colonial settlers in Australia, convict lives dominated the political and cultural landscape of the colony. Much of Australia's economic and political freedom was earned through their toil.

Drawing on the historical work of the past two decades and the 1991

fig 2   *Crudely tailored clothes, shackles, soldiers. The universal image of the 19th century transported convict.*

reinterpretation of the Hyde Park Barracks Museum by the Historic Houses Trust of New South Wales, this exhibition seeks to expand the dialogue on convicts, presenting objects and images that normalise the prisoners and their society. The achievements of male and female convict artisans are best appreciated by presenting their places of labour, viewing their products and describing their skills.

While the active role of the British military in creating and shaping Australia's social and cultural past still awaits historical advocates, its presence among the convicts is especially significant. The legal traditions of the British Army provided much of the rough justice for the colony's earliest years. Aboriginal mounted police units were formed in the Port Phillip Bay area [Victoria] to reinforce the British troops in the new colony. Army officers and enlisted men became settlers, merchants, political figures and significant landowners. The Army's discipline and strength were critical in containing the unpredictable revolts and rebellions that were commonplace among the convicts.

Inadequate rations were sure to provoke violence among the prisoners, and enormous energies were required to import, sow and harvest food crops and monitor their distribution. Adequate food was essential to prevent anarchy. Land clearance and ecological disruption on the scale required to supply the growing convict colony quickly brought the European convicts and their keepers into conflict with the Aboriginal Australians.

In the midst of this boisterous convict colony with its radically disproportionate male to female population, there was also a desire for the comfort of family. In the exhibition, the story of three convict families from Van Diemen's Land [Tasmania], New South Wales and the Swan River Colony [Western Australia], illustrate the power of companionship and nurture. Convict men and women, soldiers and settlers sought the equilibrium and security that family could bring. The quest was made more difficult by a chronic shortage of women.

Transported convict women were liberated by time and geographic displacement from the conventions of 19th century female behaviour. In the female factories and in penal colony society, they maintained an uneasy peace with their male captors. Their relative scarcity often gave them unaccustomed negotiating power; some women were able to use it, others could not.

When public opinion in Britain and Australia turned against convict transportation, a collection of Australian urban middle-class residents and workers began a struggle against an oligarchy of graziers and landowners who wanted free convict labour to continue. The exhibition concludes with an outline of the anti-transportation movement and some of its central figures. The rhetoric of revolution and active resistance to British rule that accompanied this mid-19th century Australian movement against convict banishment has never been exceeded in the nation's political life.

Convict banishment and penal settlements have a recorded history that begins with the Roman occupation of Egypt and continues to the late 20th century. Thomas More's *Utopia* (1516) describes an imaginary prison colony in the Middle East. The science fiction novelist Robert Heinlein blasts Earth's undesirables to the surface of the moon in *The Moon is a Harsh Mistress* (1966) where the lunar exiles revolt to form their own community. The international parallels of banishment, the calamities of exile and the collective struggle for equilibrium on desolate shores suggest an instinctive template for survival. David Malouf, speaking on Australia in the 1998 Boyer Lectures for the Australian Broadcasting Corporation, makes this observation:

> *We speak of these places ... as new worlds, but what they really are is the old world translated: but translated with all that implies of reinterpretation and change, not simply transported.*

This exhibition is another translation of the Australian convict experience.

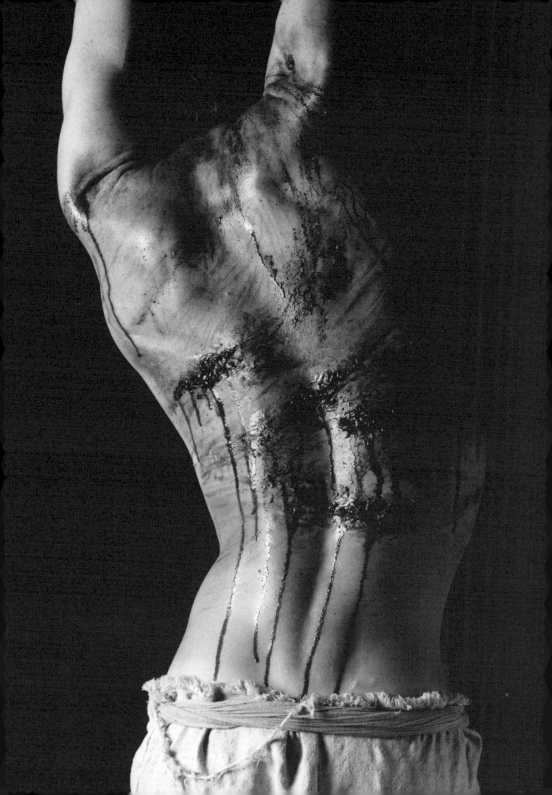

I   *The pattern of operation of penal colonies is distressingly
      consistent. Military forces usually provide order,
      rough justice and a scale of punishments ranging from
      deprivation, physical punishment and death.*

TEMPLATE
OF CRUELTY

Penal colonies are a centuries-old tradition. Operated in the classical age by the Romans, penal settlements still exist on islands owned by Italy, Mexico, Brazil and elsewhere. Beginning in the 16th century, the ascendant European powers introduced forced labour camps for political exiles and criminals throughout the world. The colonies are characterised by their geographic and physical isolation. Islands were favoured: Gibraltar, Cuba, Bermuda, Mauritius, Sakhalin, Sumatra, French Guyana, the Antilles.

For the purposes of this exhibition and its interactive computer database, a penal colony is defined as a prison outpost established by the host country for military, political, social or economic advantage. Many of the penal colonies helped lay claim to contested territory when it proved difficult to encourage free immigration to such isolated or unhealthy regions. To create these colonial beachheads, the establishing nations called upon a labour force that by virtue of its crimes, was driven into active participation. Its cooperation was ensured by military garrisons.

The pattern of operation of penal colonies is distressingly consistent. Military forces usually provide order, rough justice and a scale of punishments

fig 3   *Coercion for the rebellious convict came in many forms. Loss of privileges,
           head-shaving, the treadmill, shackles, flogging.*

ranging from deprivation, physical punishment and death. Convict work is forced and often physically taxing. Human labour generally takes the place of machinery or draft animals and time-saving machines are rare. Meals are indifferently prepared and served. The inevitable shortages ensure that for the prisoners and their keepers, food as well as clothing becomes a medium of exchange and exploitation. The colonies are largely male and when women are present, the typical population ratio of male to female is radically skewed.

The colony's banished population may consist entirely of foreign transportees and their keepers (Marias Islands, the Falkland Islands) or the convicts may appear in modest numbers among a free population (United States, Belgian Congo). The indigenous residents of these colonised lands may be ignored (Penang, Malacca) or drawn into the service of the penal colony as law-enforcers (New Caledonia, Australia). Typically, on completion of a convict's criminal sentence, or the granting of a pardon, the exile could take his or her place within the colony's society. An option to return home was available in some instances.

The labour camps established by Germany's Third Reich (1933–45) are included in this list of penal colonies because most of the camps were initially created in the German-occupied lands of Central Europe or Vichy France to force convicts to create roads, farms, buildings and factories. Many of the prisoners worked in factories and laboratories. The penal outposts often possessed geographic or political significance. In their prisoner population, types of labour, camp design and sites, uniforms and social organisation, many of the German and French camps of the 1939–45 war fit the 'Template of Cruelty'.

The listing of convict penal colonies offers a brief summary of information about known convict sites. The principal facts sought are: the dates when convicts were transported to the site; the country of origin; the agency of their transportation; and the tasks the convicts carried out at the penal settlement. The references for each site are footnoted. Researchers Jennifer Winlaw and Margaret Betteridge made major contributions to the picture and data search for this project. Additional information or images from other colonies or other authorities would be gratefully received.

One of the earliest summaries of international convict sites appeared in the volume, *Convict Workers: Reinterpreting Australia's Past*[1], edited by Stephen Nicholas. A second compilation was assembled by Michael Pearson and Duncan Marshall in their *Study of World Heritage Values: Convict Places.*[2] The list that follows, as well as the illustrated computer interactive that accompanies the exhibition, relies on the work of these scholars as a starting point.

INTERNATIONAL CONVICT SITES

Algeria   Spain transported convicts to the northern African countries of Morocco and Algeria from the 16th century until 1748. These *desterrados* (banished men) were to complete military service for Spain. At the beginning of the 18th century, *presidarios* (men sentenced to hard labour) arrived in the North African military outposts. France transported convicts to Algeria following the 1848 revolution.[3]

Andaman Islands, India   The British established a penal settlement in the Andaman Islands in 1789. As a result of the Indian Mutiny of 1857, Asian convicts from India and Burma were transported by Britain to the Andaman Islands. Approximately 12,000 convicts were sent to the Andamans.[4]

Araracuara, Colombia   The Colombian Government established an agricultural penal colony on a tributary of the Amazon River for criminals and political prisoners in 1938. It closed in 1971.[5]

Argentina (*see Tierra del Fuego*)

Asinara Island, Sardinia, Italy   From 1914 to 1918 Asinara Island, off the coast of Sardinia, was a concentration camp for thousands of Austrian–Hungarian Empire soldiers. Five thousand soldiers died on the island and were buried in a charnel house. In the 1970s Asinara became a high-security prison for transported convicts from Italy. The prison closed in 1997.[6]

Auschwitz-Birkenau, Poland   The German forced-labour camp complex, later an extermination camp (1941–45), near Cracow, used transported labour from Germany, Czechoslovakia and Poland to construct a synthetic oil and rubber factory, perform factory work, mine coal, undertake construction projects and carry out farming.[7]

Barbados, West Indies Following British occupation in 1627, 1,700 convicts were sentenced to 10-year terms to work on the tobacco plantations. There was an increase in the number of Irish convicts sent to Barbados as a result of the English Civil War of 1688. Approximately 4,000 convicts are thought to have been transported to Barbados by the 19th century.[8]

Bay Islands (Islas de la Bahia), Honduras (Belize) The site of a Spanish, and later British, penal colony, the Bay Islands initially received hostile Carib Indians from St Vincent in the early 1630s. British convicts were transported here after the Treaty of London which enabled Britain to log for mahogany.[9]

Belgian Congo, West Africa (Zaire) This was a West African colony of Belgium from 1908 (after the death of King Leopold) until 1960 when the country claimed independence as Zaire. In 1922, according to Belgian law, punishment for crime could be a four to seven year sentence as indentured labour. Convict labour was used to produce roads, railways, power stations and grow cotton, coffee and rubber.[10]

Benkoelen (Bencoolen), Sumatra The British transported Indian convicts to complete public works from 1797 to 1824. Benkoelen appears to be the first penal colony to use Indians. The colony was transferred to the Dutch in 1824.[11]

Bermuda (St George's), West Indies The British hulk, *Somerset*, arrived in 1799 and moored off Ireland Island. Between 1823 and 1863, English, Canadian and Irish courts dispatched convicts for labour in the dockyard fortifications and harbour improvements.[12]

Bonaire, Antilles Spain dispatched convicts to Bonaire from her colonies in South America. In the 17th century, Dutch ships dumped Spanish and Portuguese prisoners there to form penal settlements.[13]

Brazil The German principality Mecklenberg-Schwerin transported German prisoners to Brazil in the mid-1820s.[14] (*See also Fernando de Noronha Island.*)

British Guiana (Guyana) Guiana was first colonised by the Dutch and then by the British after 1815. Convicts were introduced in the late 1840s but they appear to be African in origin, perhaps former slaves from the British Indies. Prisoners worked at logging, building, road construction and treadmills.[15]

Burma (Myanmar)   The British transported Indian convicts to Burma after 1826. These sites were also used for transshipments of Burmese convicts to the Straits Settlements.[16]

Buru Island, Indonesia   Buru Island was established in 1969 as a penal colony by the Sukarno-led government. Convicts transported to Buru were political criminals and included the novelist Pramoedya Ananta Toer who was exiled here for ten years. Logging and agriculture were the colony's primary activities. Its present status is unknown.[17]

Capraia Island, Italy   Since 1872, approximately one-third of this small island near Elba has been used as an agricultural penal colony by the Italian Government.[18]

Cape Breton Island, Canada   In 1786, to ease Britain's convict population pressure, a suggestion was made to send the convicts to labour in the salt mines on Cape Breton Island. This plan was rejected, but in 1789 Cape Breton Island received Irish convicts who had been refused entry into Quebec. The convicts were dumped and their fate is unknown.[19]

Cape of Good Hope (Southern Africa)   The Cape Colony of the Netherlands received banished convicts from the Asian locations of the Dutch East Indian Company from about 1655 to 1795. Among these convicts were Dutch criminals from the East Indies, Asian slaves, and Chinese traders and labourers.[20]

Equatorial Guinea, West Africa   Equatorial Guinea was ceded by Portugal to Spain in the late 18th century. In 1865, there was a serious labour shortage on the coffee plantations and Spain considered importing Chinese and Filipino labour, but instead decided to transport Cuban convicts to work on the plantations from 1879. In 1898, after losing control of Cuba in the Spanish–American War, Spain sent her convicts to Morocco. Equatorial Guinea claimed independence in 1968.[21]

Falkland Islands   The Falkland Islands have been continually contested by the Spanish, French and British and consequently there have been many abortive attempts at settlement on the Falklands. Between 1826 and 1831 the British Falklands settlement sought to supplement its labour force by introducing Indian convicts.[22]

Fernando de Noronha Island, Brazil Portugal transported convicts to the island in the 19th century. It remains an active penal site.[23]

French Guyana, South America The French Government began to send criminals to French Guyana in 1852. French Guyana was an active penal site for French political prisoners and Algerians between 1852 and 1939. The last prisoner was released in 1953. Approximately 70,000 prisoners passed through French Guyana.[24]

Ghana (Cape Coast Castle), West Africa Convicts were sent here in two groups in February 1782 as a British experiment in convict transportation. Less than 30 convicts out of 212 are known to have survived. It has been suggested that Ghana was dismissed as a possible penal site due to concerns that the 'natives' would ally with the convicts and help destroy the forts.[25]

Gibraltar British convicts were transported here (1842–75) to construct breakwaters and forts. Most returned to Britain after completing their sentences. Some of these prisoners were transported to Australia in 1848.[26]

Gross-Rosen, Silesia, Germany One of Germany's largest forced-labour camps, Gross-Rosen (1940–45) used Jews and prisoners of many nations in the granite quarry, the Krups armament factories, chemical manufacture, wireless equipment and textile production. The camps were guarded by German convicts. Approximately 78,000 people were sent to Gross-Rosen and 40,000 people perished.[27]

Guyana (see British Guiana and French Guyana)

Hainan Island, China Hainan Island, located in the South China Sea, has been a site of exile for centuries, most notably for the 11th-century dissident poet Su Dongpo.[28]

Havana, Cuba Convicts were sent to Havana from Spain and Mexico. The Spanish convicts had been convicted of military crimes such as desertion. Convicts from Mexico were civilians. Prison terms fluctuated in the 1770s from six to eight years. The convicts were sent to reconstruct and strengthen fortifications, notably after 1767. In Havana, the convict population averaged 2,000.[29]

Hawaii In 1824, Hawaii's Queen declared the island of Kaho'olawe a place of banishment for men. Women were exiled to the island of Lana'i.

These two islands received convicts between 1828 and 1853.[30]

Janowska, Ukraine This forced-labour and extermination camp was established in the suburbs of Lvov (1941–43), in the USSR, with transportees from the German-occupied regions of Central Europe. Inmates were forced to undertake tasks with no practical purpose, such as digging trenches or moving loads about the camp.[31]

Kaiserwald, Latvia The first inmates to this German forced-labour camp (1943–44) near Riga were transported German convicts. They worked on the German railway system in vehicle maintenance and electrical works. In July 1944, all inmates except those between the ages of 18 and 30 were killed. Approximately 12,000 Jews from Latvia, Poland and Hungary were also incarcerated.[32]

Koh Tao, Thailand This small island was used by Thailand as a banishment site for political prisoners until 1940.[33]

Kolyma Complex, Siberia, Russia A part of 'the Gulag Archipelago' made infamous by Alexander Solzhenitsyn, Kolyma was situated in the north-east corner of the USSR, and active under Stalin between 1932 and 1954. Approximately three million people perished at Kolyma as they mined for gold under the ice. Approximately 6 per cent of convicts were women. Many primary accounts of the harsh Kolyma regime survive.[34]

Malacca, Malaysia Transportation from Ceylon and northern India lasted from the late 1700s to the mid-1800s. Between 1805 and 1808, 100 Indian convicts were transported by the British for public works. In 1826, Penang, Malacca and Singapore were united by the British to form the Straits Settlements.[35]

Marias Islands, Mexico Four dry islands off the western coast of Mexico near Guadalajara are largely uninhabited except for a government penal colony on one island. Marias Islands exports include guano, salt and lumber.[36]

Mauritius Between the 1630s and 1710, Batavian (Indonesian) and Chinese convicts were transported to Mauritius by the Dutch. From 1816 to 1837, the British transported Indian convicts from Bengal and Bombay to construct public works and undertake agricultural work. Between 1819 and 1835, Sri

fig 4   *(overleaf) New Caledonia, like many other penal colonies, was an island prison imposed on unsuspecting indigenous occupants.*

Lankan convicts were also transported. In total, approximately 1,500 prisoners were transported.[37]

Mons Claudianus, Egypt An Egyptian penal colony established by the Romans near Port Safaga, this site was active in Hadrian's reign (117–138 AD). Material quarried in Mons Claudianus is still visible in Roman buildings.[38]

Moreton Bay, (Brisbane, Queensland) A convict settlement was first established at Redcliffe in 1824 on the western shore of Moreton Bay. It was planned as a penal outpost for convicts under secondary sentences. The site proved unsuitable and the colony moved up the river to the location of present-day Brisbane. Convicts were held there from 1824 to 1839, when the area was opened for free settlement.

Morocco, North Africa Spain transported convicts to the North African *presidios* (Spanish military colonies) from the 16th century. The *presidios* increased greatly in population after the abolition of the rowing galleys in 1748. The convicts were to labour on the fortifications as the colonies came under incessant attack in the 18th century. All supplies came irregularly from Spain and food rations often consisted only of bread.[39]

Natzweiler, France The Natzweiler-Struthof forced-labour camp (1941–44) was 50 kilometres from Strasbourg in south-eastern France. Three hundred German convicts were initially sent to Natzweiler, followed by members of the French Resistance, Jews and Gypsies. The convicts laboured in the quarry and armaments factories.[40]

New Brunswick, Canada In April 1842, Lord Stanley of Britain's Home Office proposed a scheme for transporting juvenile offenders from Parkhurst Prison, the Isle of Wight, to New Brunswick. The correspondence indicates that 'small parties' of 'pardoned' juveniles were sent to New Brunswick as so-called free emigrants.[41]

New Caledonia France transported political and criminal prisoners to New Caledonia from 1863 to around 1896. The prisoners were employed on public works. Political prisoners from French Algeria were also transported in the 1870s.[42]

Newfoundland, Canada There was unregulated and speculative British transportation of Irish convicts to Newfoundland in the 1780s.[43]

New South Wales The decision to establish a penal colony at Botany Bay closely followed the loss of Britain's American colonies after 1776. In 1788 a fleet of 11 ships, carrying over 700 convict men and women, arrived in the country. By the time transportation to New South Wales technically ceased in 1840, over 80,000 men and women had entered the colony under sentence.

New Zealand In 1842, The British Home Office outlined a scheme to transport juvenile prisoners from Parkhurst Prison, Isle of Wight, to Britain's Pacific colonies. A group of convicted juveniles was transported to New Zealand and on arrival, the young convicts were required to take out closely supervised apprenticeships. The transportation of 56 children is noted in April 1842 in the Colonial Office correspondence, although there are references to other Parkhurst shipments to New Zealand.[44]

Nicobar Islands The Nancowry Harbour penal settlement was established by the British using convicts from Andaman Islands between 1869 and 1888. *(See Andaman Islands.)*

Norfolk Island A penal settlement was established on Norfolk Island in 1788 as an outpost to the main New South Wales colony. An attempt to establish a flax industry failed and the colony was abandoned in 1813. The island was reoccupied in 1825 as a place of secondary punishment for troublesome convicts. The penal establishment was finally closed in 1856.

Nova Scotia, Canada There was unregulated and speculative British transportation of Irish criminals to Nova Scotia in the 1780s. Haphazard supervision resulted in numerous Irish convicts returning to Ireland.[45]

Pantelleria Island, Italy The island was a place of banishment in ancient Roman times from 217 BC to 700 AD. Between the 12th and 16th centuries the island was in the possession of Spain, Turkey and Italy. Located off the south-west coast of Sicily, it remains the site of an Italian penal colony.[46]

Penang, Malaysia Between 1796 and 1860, Penang annually received Indian convicts transported by the British Government. The convicts built Fort Cornwallis, and Penang became part of the colonial network of the Straits Settlements.[47]

Pianosa Island, Italy An agricultural penal colony south of the island of Elba was established in 1856 by the Italian Government. It was also a place of banishment in the Roman Era.[48]

Plaszow, Poland Situated near Cracow, this forced-labour camp was active between 1942 and 1944. Plaszow was guarded by Ukrainian Nazis. Considered a satellite camp of Auschwitz, Plaszow received German convicts, Polish Jews, Gypsies and other nationalities.[49]

Port Phillip (Melbourne, Victoria) The first attempt to establish an outpost on Port Phillip Bay was in Sorrento in 1803. This site was abandoned less than a year later. The plan was revived again in Westernport Bay in 1826 and failed the following year. Pastoral land was sought in the region in the 1830s and settlement began in earnest. Convict gangs were used to clear scrub, construct roads and erect government buildings. When transportation ceased in 1849–50, at least 2,500 convicts had been sent to Port Phillip from Britain and New South Wales.

Qinghai, China The high mountain plateau of Qinghai has been described as China's gulag where, in the 20th century, prisoners laboured in factories and on farms. Although precise dates are not available, data suggests that convict transportation began around 1950 and declined in the 1980s.[50]

Queensland (see Moreton Bay)

Rara Avis, Costa Rica An inactive penal colony in the jungle near Rio Frio, this colony was established by the national government. No dates are available.[51]

Robben Island, South Africa Initially a Dutch penal colony, the island was later used by the British Government for the same purposes. In 1833, the British Government decided that African slaves sentenced to transportation should be sent to Robben Island. Between 1846 and 1931, the island was used as a leper colony. Between 1960 and 1991, Robben Island was administered as a prison to punish those who opposed apartheid. Nationalist leader Nelson Mandela served much of his 20-year sentence for political offences on Robben Island. In 1997, as President, he opened the island as a museum.[52]

Sakhalin Island, Russia Russian writer Anton Chekhov publicised the terrible condition of the convicts of Sakhalin Island after a visit to the colony in 1897.

fig 5   *On Sakhalin Island, Russian convicts took the place of beasts of burden. This was*
commonplace in penal settlements.

Chekhov visited the islands with official permission and published a book
about his experiences five years later. Over two million political prisoners
were transported to Siberia and Sakhalin Island from 1820 to 1920.[53]

San Cristobal (Chatham Island), Equador   Once under the control of Spain, the
easternmost island in the Galapagos Islands group in the Pacific Ocean has
long been used as a government penal colony. No dates are available.[54]

San Juan, Puerto Rico Transported Spanish and North African convicts
were used in Spanish fortifications and public works at San Juan, especially
after 1767. The average Puerto Rican convict population was 476 workers,
however 10 per cent were ill at any one time. Convicts from other Spanish
colonies in Central America were allowed to settle here after serving their
sentences.[55]

Siberia, Russia *(see also the Solovetky Islands and Kolyma Complex)* Although the
study of convict transportation in Russia is in its infancy, over two million

political prisoners were transported to Siberia and Sakhalin Island from 1820 to 1920. The transportation of political prisoners did not cease until the collapse of the USSR in the 1980s. Civil criminals are still transported today. Convicts from Russian territories and Russian allies were also transported to Siberia: the Grand Duchy of Finland, under Russian rule in the 19th century, transported both male and female prisoners; and North Korea transported male convicts to work as labour gangs (1974–84) on the Trans-Siberian Baikal-Amur Mainline railway (BAM) to repay Soviet Cold War fiscal debts.[56]

Singapore, The Republic of Singapore   Indian convicts were transported to Singapore by the British from 1826 to 1867 and employed in public works. During the 1830s, 90 per cent of Indian convicts returned to their homeland after serving their sentences. This followed an offer from the Indian Government to pay the return passage. The British also transported Chinese convict labourers from Hong Kong between 1847 and 1856.[57]

Solovetsky Islands, Russia   Isolated from the mainland by ice floes, the Solovetsky Islands in the Baltic Sea were initially colonised in the 15th century by monks. Ivan the Terrible (1530–84) activated the islands as a penal colony for convicts from the Ukraine. The islands, which continued in use until 1905, were infamous for their bleak, unventilated caves. They were reactivated as a penal colony in the 1920s.[58]

Spanish Guinea, West Africa (*see Equatorial Guinea*)

Swan River Colony (Fremantle, Western Australia)   A free British settlement was established on the Swan River in 1826. By 1840, economic collapse seemed imminent and convict transportation was requested by the colonists in the late 1840s to provide labour for public works as well as stimulate the local market. Approximately 9,700 male convicts were sent to Western Australia from 1850 until transportation ceased in 1868.

Tierra del Fuego   A penal colony was established in these remote islands by Argentina in 1884. In 1902, the Argentine transportees were consolidated near the new town of Ushuaia. The colony was intended to provide labour for public works as well as populate the islands. Prisoners were encouraged to settle after serving their sentences. An early study of the Tierra del Fuego penal colony by Roberto Payro was titled *La Australia Argentina* (1898).[59]

United States of America   As Britain's foremost colony in the Americas, over 50,000 convicts were transported to the north-east coast of America after 1640. The Revolutionary War ended transportation in 1776. Attempts were made by the British to resume transportation to the United States after the peace in 1783–84 but the convict cargoes were rejected at their destinations. The British transported US citizens to Van Diemen's Land in the late 1830s after capturing them during skirmishes on the Canadian border.[60]

Van Diemen's Land (Tasmania)   Fearing French designs on Van Diemen's Land, Britain established a penal colony there in 1803. When transportation ceased in 1852, 67,000 convicts had been transported to the settlement. The island population was later active in its opposition to convict transportation and it was renamed Tasmania in 1855.

Veracruz, Mexico (see Havana and San Juan) Spanish and North African convicts transported to Veracruz by Spain were used in as labour fortifications and public works, especially after 1767.[61]

Victoria (see Port Phillip Bay)

Western Australia (see Swan River Colony)

ENDNOTES

1   Steven Nicholas (ed.), *Convict Workers: Reinterpreting Australia's Past*, Cambridge University Press, Cambridge, 1988.

2   Michael Pearson and Duncan Marshall, *Study of World Heritage Values: Convict Places*, Commonwealth Department of the Environment, Sport and Territories, 1995.

3   Ruth Pike, *Penal Servitude in Early Modern Spain*, The University of Wisconsin Press, Madison, 1983, pp.41–42. Nicholas, *Convict Workers*, p.34.

4   RC Majumdar, *Penal Settlement in the Andamans*, Gazetteers Unit, Department of Culture, Ministry of Federal and Social Welfare, Delhi, 1975, p.47, p.64. David Mackay, *A Place of Exile: The European Settlement of New South Wales*, Oxford University Press, Melbourne, 1985, p.86. Priten Roy and Swapnesh Choudhury, *Cellular Jail*, Farsight Publishers, Dehli, 1998.

5   Tropenbos Foundation, <tropenbos@iac.agro.nl>, November 1996. M Losada, *La Prision del Raudal*, Instituto Colombiano de Antropologia, Columbia, 1998.

6   <http://whc.unesco.org/en/ tentativelists>, April 2008.

7   Israel Gutman (ed.), *Encyclopedia of the Holocaust*, Vol. 2, Vol. 3, Macmillan Publishing Company, New York, 1990. *Auschwitz: Nazi Extermination Camp*, Interpress Publishers, Warsaw, 1975.

8   HM Beckles, *White Servitude and Black Slavery in Barbados, 1627–1715*, The University of Tennessee Press, Knoxville, 1989, pp.5–23.

9   ON Bolland, *The Formation of a Colonial Society: Belize, from Conquest to Crown Colony*, The John Hopkins University Press, Baltimore, 1977, p.25, p.32.

10   LH Gann and Peter Duignan, *The Rulers of Belgian Africa 1884–1914*, Princeton University Press, Princeton, 1979, p.218.

11   Nicholas, *Convict Workers*, pp.32–33.

12   Roger Willock, *Bulwark of Empire: Bermuda's Fortified Naval Base 1860–1920*, privately published, 1962, p.74.

13 <www.interknowledge.com/bonaire/bonhisol.htm>, January 1999. This information is based on this secondary source.

14 Nicholas, *Convict Workers*, p.36.

15 Sir Henry Light, 'Observations in regard to Penal Settlements and Prisons in British Guiana', 9 July 1848, attached to correspondence from Earl Grey to Lieutenant Governor Walker, 22 July 1848, *Historical Records of Australia*, Series 1, Vol. 26, p.581.

16 Roy and Choudhury, *Cellular Jail*, pp.16–18. N Rajendra, 'Transmarine Convicts in the Straits Settlements,' *Asian Profile*, Vol. 11:5, October 1983, p.509.

17 PA Toer, *The Mute's Soliloquy*, Hyperion, New York, 1999. Carmel Budiardjo, *Surviving Indonesia's Gulag: A Western Woman Tells Her Story*, Cassell, London, 1996.

18 *Encyclopaedia Britannica*, 1996.

19 Wilfred Oldham, *Britain's Convicts to the Colonies*, Library of Australian History, Sydney, 1990, pp.111–112.

20 Kerry Ward, 'Bandietin and Bannelingen: Penal and Political Transportation in the Dutch East India Company's Indian Ocean Empire 1655–1795' in *Colonial Places, Convict Spaces: Penal Transportation in Global Context c1600–1940*, conference papers, University of Leicester, December, 1999.

21 Max Liniger-Goumaz, *Small is not always Beautiful: The Story of Equatorial Guinea*, C Hurst & Company, London, 1988, p.22, p.44.

22 IJ Strange, *The Falkland Islands*, David & Charles, London, 1981, p.54.

23 *Encyclopaedia Britannica*, 1996.

24 Colin Foster, *France and Botany Bay: The Lure of a Penal Colony*, Melbourne University Press, Melbourne, 1996, p.1, p.159–161.

25 Oldham, *Britain's Convicts to the Colonies*. AGL Shaw, *Convicts and the Colonies: A Study of Penal Transportation from Great Britain and Ireland to Australia and other parts of the British Empire*, Melbourne University Press, Melbourne, 1966, p.43.

26 J Blom-Cooper, *A Prison 1000 Years Old*, Howard League for Penal Reform, London, 1982.

27 Gutman (ed.), *Encyclopedia of the Holocaust*, Vol. 3, p.623.

28 Liam D'Arcy Brown, *Green Dragon, Sombre Warrior: A Journey around China's Symbolic Frontiers*, John Murray, London, 2003.

29 Pike, *Penal Servitude in Early Modern Spain*, p.145.

30 <http://www.2.hawaii.edu/~vbadua/history.html>, May 1998, Rowland Reeve, 'Historic References to the Penal Colony on Kaho'olawe', [Prepared for the Historic Houses Trust of NSW] 1997, p.2.

31 Gutman (ed.), *Encyclopedia of the Holocaust*, Vol. 2, Vol. 3, p.733.

32 Gutman (ed.), *Encyclopedia of the Holocaust*, Vol. 2, Vol. 3, p.777.

33 <http://www.kohtao.com/>, 1998. This information has been based on this secondary source.

34 Robert Conquest, *Kolyma: The Arctic Death Camps*, Macmillan, Hong Kong, 1978, pp.14–17. Varlam Shalamov, *Kolyma Tales*, Norton, New York, 1980, pp.7–17.

35 SH Holt, *Old Malacca*, Oxford University Press, Kuala Lumpur, 1993. Nicholas, *Convict Workers*, p.32.

36 *Encyclopaedia Britannica*, 1996. <http://www.ucol.mx/ocean/pproj.html>, November 1997.

37 Clare Anderson, *Convicts in the Indian Ocean: Transportation from South Asia to Mauritius, 1815–53*, St Martin's Press, New York, 2000. Ian Duffield and James Bradley (eds.), *Representing Convicts: New Perspectives on Convict Forced Labour Migration*, Leicester University Press, London, 1997, p.164. *Index to Dispatches from the Governor of Ceylon to the Secretary of State for the Colonies*, National Archives, Colombo, Sri Lanka.

38 <http://interoz.com/egypt/mons_claudianus.html>, May 1998.

39 Pike, *Penal Servitude in Early Modern Spain*, p.115.

40 Gutman (ed.), *Encyclopedia of the Holocaust*, Vol. 2, Vol. 3, pp.1038–1039.

41 Governor Gipps Dispatches, April, May, 1842, ML A1288, State Library of New South Wales.

42 Foster, *France and Botany Bay*, pp.172–174.

43 Jed Martin, 'Convict Transportation to Newfoundland in 1789', *Acadiensis*, Vol. V, No. 1, Autumn, 1975, pp.84–99.

44   Governor Gipps Dispatches, April, May, 1842.
45   Martin, 'Convict Transportation to Newfoundland in 1789', p.89.
46   <libeccio@libeccio.it>, 1997. *Encyclopaedia Britannica*, 1996.
47   Nicholas, *Convict Workers*, p.32.
48   *Encyclopaedia Britannica*, 1996.
49   Gutman (ed.), *Encyclopedia of the Holocaust*, Vol. 2, Vol. 3, pp.1139–1140.
50   *Laogai Handbook*, <http://www.laogai.org/hdbook/qinghai.htm>, April 2008. Jan Wong, *Red
      China Blues: My Long March from Mao to Now*, Doubleday, Sydney, 1996. Harry Wu, *Bitter
      Winds: A Memoir of My Years in China's Gulag*, John Wiley, New York, 1993.
51   <www.interlog.com/~rainfrst/rara-avis/factsheet.html>. This information has been based on this
      secondary source.
52   Col. Sec. Office, Port Louis, 28 September 1833 to Commissary of Police, Mitchell Library
      Z2A/72. *Robben Island*, Robben Island Recreational Club, nd. *Encyclopedia Britannica*, 1996.
53   Anton Chekhov, *The Islands of Sakhalin* [1895], The Folio Society, London, 1989 [reprint of
      1895 edition], p.2. Simon Karlinsky and MH Heim (eds.), *Anton Chekhov's Life and Thought:
      Selected Letters and Commentary*, Northwestern University Press, Evanston, 1997 edition.
54   *Encyclopaedia Britannica*, 1996.
55   Pike, *Penal Servitude in Early Modern Spain*, pp.138–139.
56   Tomas Kotkas, 'The 19th-century Deportation of Finnish Convicts to Siberia' in *Colonial Places,
      Convict Spaces: Penal Transportation in Global Context c1600–1940* conference papers. Gregory
      Feifer, 'In Russia's Far East, North Koreans Labor Quietly', National Public Radio [transcript],
      13 April 2008, <http://www.npr.org/templates/story/story?storyId=89323218>, April 2008. NB
      Lincoln, *Conquest of a Continent: Siberia and the Russians*, Random House, 1994. Alexander
      Solzhenitsyn, *The Gulag Archipelago*, Vol. I–VII, Harper & Row, New York, 1974–1978. Giles
      Whittell, 'Gulags repay North Korea Debt', *The Australian*, 7 August 2001, p.10.
57   Nicholas, *Convict Workers*, p.33. Rajendra, 'Transmarine Convicts in the Straits Settlements'.
58   S Pidhainy, *Islands of Death*, Burns & MacEachern, Toronto, 1953, pp.5–10.
59   CP Vairo, *El Presidio de Ushuaia* [The Prison of Ushuaia], Zagier & Urruty Publications, Buenos
      Aires, 1997.
60   A Roger Ekirch, *Bound for America*, Clarendon Press, Oxford, 1987. Cassandra Pybus and
      Hamish Maxwell-Stewart, *American Citizens and British Slaves: Yankee Political Prisoners in an
      Australian Penal Colony 1839–1850*, Melbourne University Press, Melbourne, 2000.
61   Pike, *Penal Servitude in Early Modern Spain*, pp.138–139.

2   *To ascend the Holborn Hill scaffold near Hyde Park was*
to mount 'the three-legged mare' or 'the three-legged stool'
for a 'Hanging Match'. Ultimately, to hang at the Tyburn
gallows was to 'Dance the Paddington Frisk', to 'Morris'
or 'Dance upon Nothing at the Sheriff's Ball'.

THE GREAT
FEAR

Transportation was exile. It was a fierce punishment that ejected men, women and children from their homelands into distant and unknown territories. The expulsion of criminals from the British Isles to England's North American and Caribbean colonies, Gibraltar and Australia was a desperate measure that was symptomatic of the commonly perceived lawlessness of Britain's cities. The banishment of convicts began in Britain in the 17th century and continued until the mid-19th century.

In the era of British transportation, criminal punishment was often a public spectacle. Stocks, floggings, brandings and frequent public hangings were intended as dramatic deterrents for potential criminals. But despite sentences of public executions meted out to 678 criminals at London's Old Bailey from 1749 to 1771, a current of fear continued to flow through British cities and towns.[1] English popular prints and literature of the period illustrate an entrenched public perception of pandemic criminal behaviour.

Driven by ever-increasing hysteria, even minor crimes against property began to draw more extreme penalties from magistrates. In 1826 alone, there were 1,203 death sentences passed in England and Wales.[2] Yet, despite

fig 6   *Hogarth's print satirises England's addiction to gin. The openly dissolute woman*
demonstrates the depth of social decay.

the cavalcade of victims to the gallows, a jaunty indifference to criminal behaviour began to surface among city-dwellers. Naturally, this validated the anxiety of property owners. From 1688 to 1820, the number of capital offences in British law rose from approximately 50 to over 200. And despite the terrible deterrents, murderers, pickpockets and highwaymen became celebrated public figures.

A sampling of these dissolute fictional and non-fictional characters demonstrates something of their continuing popularity: Molly Brazen; The Artful Dodger; Spring-Heel Jack; Johnathan Wilde; McHeath; Crook-Finger'd Jack; Nimmin' Ned; Sweeney Todd; Fagin; Sukey Tawdrey; Abel Magwitch and Half-hanged Smith. Smith, a packer, soldier and sailor, was hung for two hours at Tyburn in 1709, but when he was cut down, Half-hanged Smith was found to be alive. He was reprieved.[3]

The thief Dauntless Dick Turpin (hanged 1739), the highwayman Jack Sheppard (hanged 1724) and the London hangman Jack Ketch were near-mythical figures whose careers were continued in song and prose long after their deaths. Their deeds inspired plays such as John Gay's *Beggar's Opera* (1727), and novels such as Daniel Defoe's *Moll Flanders* (1722), as well as operas and ballads. Defoe himself was no stranger to prison, having served one year in 1703–04.

As the tempo of the gallows-drop (gibbet in popular slang) increased, the public enthusiasm for the 'Sheriff's Ball' at Tyburn grew to riotous proportions. The text of a printed waybill for the hanging of the robber Johnathan Wilde illustrates some of the ironic pleasures of criminal executions.

> *To all the Thieves, Whores, Pickpockets, Family Fellons,*
> *etc. in Great Britain and Ireland. Gentlemen & Ladies.*
> *You are hereby desir'd to accompany yr worthy friend ye*
> *pious Mr Johnathan Wild from his Seat at Whittington*
> *Colledge to ye Tripple Tree where he is to make his last*
> *Exit ... Pray bring this Ticket with you.*[4]

Popular prints and illustrations reflecting the mayhem of the city streets also flourished. These visual impressions of crime and misery were as important as literature in shaping the mood of British society. The prints show satirical scenes of street brawls (Thomas Rowlandson: *The Miseries of*

fig 7   *The dense population of London was the wonder of the world. Critics described the*
          city as 'Babylon' or the 'Great Wen'.

London), the corruption of youth (George Cruikshank: *Teaching the Young to
Shoot, Smoke, Drink, Fight, Cheat*), dissolution and drunkenness (Thomas
Hogarth: *Gin Lane*) and the ever-present threat of transportation to Botany
Bay (George Cruikshank: *A Startling Interrogation*). Amusing though these
prints may be, satire is traditionally a constructive device of denouncement.
The energy the artists brought to their illustrations suggests some of their
cynical concerns at the imagined lawlessness of the era.

   While there is no doubt that hanging spectacles were clarifying events
that crudely focused public attention on the immutable link between crime
and punishment, the well-documented vernacular language of British cities
suggests that these open-air processions and executions became an accepted
and entertaining feature of the urban landscape.

   It was a 'Theatre of the Absurd'. To ascend the Holborn Hill scaffold
near Hyde Park was to mount 'the three-legged mare' or 'the three-legged
stool' for a 'Hanging Match'. Ultimately, to hang at the Tyburn gallows was
to 'Dance the Paddington Frisk', to 'Morris' or 'Dance upon Nothing at the

Sheriff's Ball'. Eric Partridge's *Dictionary of the Underworld* (Routledge & Kegan Paul, 1950) is a rich source of 'flash talk'. Peter Linebaugh's chapter 'The Tyburn Riot against the Surgeons' in Douglas Hay, et al., *Albion's Fatal Tree, Crime and Society in 18th Century Britain*, Pantheon, 1975 also summarises some of this slang gleaned from the literature of the era.

The persistent critics of the public hanging pageants at Tyburn in London won a victory when Tyburn executions were discontinued in 1783 and the spectacles were transferred to the city's Newgate Prison. While the executions were now performed inside the prison walls where force could easily be mustered, they remained public events.

Despite the effort to suppress the civil unrest attending public hangings, the prose treatment of crime continued to grow at a considerable rate. A scurrilous publication, the so-called *Newgate Calendar, or, Malefactors' Bloody Register*, provided a compendium of criminal biographies. It first appeared in 1773 and soon grew to five volumes of gory deeds. Its closest competitor, *Annals of Newgate* (1775) was equally sensational. In the early 19th century, the publishers, encouraged by lower excise taxes on printed material, rushed into print with *The Lives of the Most Notorious Highwaymen, Footpads, etc.* (1836), *The Calendar of Horrors* (1836) and ultimately, *The Body-Snatchers* (1845).

These notorious celebrants of crime ultimately created a new literary genre, the infamous 'Penny Dreadful', to satisfy the public's pleasure in crime and its attendant punishments. The 'Penny Dreadfuls' were crudely printed, illustrated and bound booklets that contained extraordinary fictions that formed an encyclopedia of aberrant behaviour including petty crime (*Paul the Poacher*), cannibalism (*Sweeny Todd, the Demon Barber*) and moral mayhem (*The Merry Wives of London*). The subject matter and its readership provides startling insights into mid-19th century British reading habits.

The popularity of the 'Penny Dreadful' soon caught the eye of more sophisticated publishers. Writers such as Walter Scott (*Rob Roy*) and Charles Dickens began to provide serial novels on criminal subjects in British popular magazines. This also constituted a new literary genre, the so-called 'Newgate Novel' after London's most notorious gaol. Dickens wrote so authoritatively on crime and its milieu that his world of thieves, transportees and murderers continues, in the 20th century, to represent 19th century England.

Dickens's skill resounds in this brief excerpt from *Oliver Twist*:

'Stop Thief! Stop Thief!' There is a magic in the sound.
The tradesman leaves his counter, and the carman his
waggon; the butcher throws down his tray, the baker his
basket, the milkman his pail, the errand-boy his parcels,
the schoolboy his marbles ... Away they run, pell-mell,
helter-skelter, slap-dash, tearing, yelling, screaming...

The public appetite for crime, punishment, fear and terror seemed insatiable during the period of British convict transportation. Few recall that from Queen Victoria's marriage in 1840, there were seven attempts on her life. But as British 19th century social reforms began to take effect, new wonders such as steam, factories and mechanised wars began to monopolise the public mind. Hangings became fewer. New forms of punishment became more furtive, secretive, concealing and isolating.

ENDNOTES

1   John Howard, *The State of the Prisons in England and Wales with Preliminary Observations and an Account of some Foreign Prisons*, Warrington, Printed By William Eyres, 1777, p.482.
2   GR Porter, *The Progress of the Nation in its various Social and Economical Relations from the Beginning of the 19th Century to the Present Time*, London, 1843, p.178.
3   Peter Linebaugh, 'The Tyburn Riot Against the Surgeons', in Douglas Hay et al., *Albion's Fatal Tree: Crime and Society in 18th Century Britain*, Pantheon, 1975, p.103.
4   Facsimile reproduced in Hay et al., *Albion's Fatal Tree*, Figure 6.

3 *The penalties exacted in these lonely Australian sites were psychological as well as physical. And far from the gaze of the Sydney-based Governors, these majestic sites could be subject to exponential misrule.*

VANISHMENT

'Humanity probably invented exile first and prison later. Expulsion from the tribe, was, of course, exile', the famous 20th century writer and convict Alexander Solzhenitsyn once wrote. 'We were quick to realise how difficult it is for a man to exist, divorced from his own place, his familiar territory. Everything is wrong and awkward...'[1]

In the 1780s, relatively little was known of the land that the world called New Holland. In May 1787, a fleet of 11 ships left Spithead, off the Isle of Wight, with a cargo of 750 convicts for Botany Bay. The fleet's goal was distance; sea miles between its cargo and Britain.

While the Aboriginal Australians watched from the edge of the trees, the British paced out their European convict colony in Sydney Cove in January 1788. Within a month, this European foothold was extended by a party of convict men and women under the command of naval Lieutenant Philip Gidley King. The party was sent to occupy deserted Norfolk Island some 1,670 kilometres off the east coast of the continent. Here, the convicts were put to work cultivating flax and corn and harvesting the Norfolk Island pines for ship's masts and spars.[2] Norfolk Island was considered a strategic

fig 8 *Near-impenetrable forests and vast oceans were as effective for containment as iron bars and shackles.*

location for securing naval stores of timber and cordage.

Within a few years, a succession of British Navy and Army Governors secured the economic and social future of England's new convict settlement at Port Jackson. Despite the chronic shortage of supplies, the colony's military masters cautiously extended their convict labour force into Van Diemen's Land [Tasmania], Melville Island [Northern Territory], Moreton Bay [Queensland], Port Phillip [Victoria], and the Swan River Settlement [Western Australia]. By the time convict transportation to Australia ceased in 1868, over 160,000 convict men and women had been banished from England, Ireland and the British colonies. Few returned.

Convicts who reoffended in the colony often had their sentences extended. Some were banished to even more remote locations within Australia; this meant that a convict could be twice exiled. Penal settlements multiplied as the pressure of an ever-expanding population and a transportation network penetrated the original isolation.

Many of the locations chosen for Australian exile for secondary offenders possessed a wild beauty that poets and painters of the era would have described as sublime. Macquarie Harbour on the stormy western coast of Van Diemen's Land; Maria Island in the Tasman Sea; remote Norfolk Island in the Pacific Ocean; and Fort Dundas on Melville Island in the Timor Sea were places of great natural beauty. Yet to an unschooled eye, the unknown flora, fauna and Aboriginal inhabitants of these desolate stations became a source of terror. The penalties exacted in these lonely areas were psychological as well as physical. And far from the gaze of the Sydney-based Governors, these majestic locations could be subject to exponential misrule.

THE PRINCIPAL SITES OF BANISHMENT
Botany Bay / Port Jackson, New South Wales (1788) Following the 1770 charts of Captain James Cook, the First Fleet of convicts, civilians and military keepers sailed to New Holland. After examining Botany Bay, the Commander of the fleet and first Governor of the penal colony, Captain Arthur Phillip, chose to shift the colony to Sydney Cove, Port Jackson. Sydney remained a penal settlement until transportation was officially ended in 1840. The last convicts were turned out of the Hyde Park Convict Barracks in 1848.

fig 9   *The soldiers that supervised the convicts' journey to New South Wales were the prisoners' constant companions.*

Norfolk Island (1789) Navy Lieutenant Philip Gidley King established a settlement called Sydney on this island with a small group of about 20 convicts and staff. This first settlement was abandoned in 1813 and the buildings destroyed to prevent use by future occupants. In 1825, the island was reoccupied as a place of secondary punishment for incorrigible prisoners. After transportation to New South Wales was technically suspended in 1840, Norfolk Island continued to receive transported felons from Great Britain as well as recidivist criminals from the mainland colonies. The penal settlement closed in 1856.

Hobart, Van Diemen's Land (1803) Risdon Cove on the Derwent River near Hobart was the first British settlement on this island in the Southern Ocean. Although it was initially conceived as a colony for free settlers, male and female convicts were required for agriculture, domestic service and public works. However, within 16 years, the convict population had risen to 70 per cent of the total population. Convict transportation to Van Diemen's Land

fig 10   *The convicts built a number of major buildings in the Moreton Bay penal settlement. Only two survive.*

was suspended in 1852 and the last convict ship arrived in 1853. The island was renamed Tasmania in 1855.

Newcastle, New South Wales (1804) A penal settlement at the so-called 'Coal River' (now the Hunter River) was established in 1804 as a place of secondary punishment. The site was later renamed Newcastle. Repeat offenders were employed in coal mines, cedar-cutting and recovering sea salt. The most incorrigible prisoners were required to produce lime from the burning of seashells. However, in a short time, free settlers from Sydney moved into the area and more distant settlements were required. Its role as a penal settlement was over by 1824.

Port Macquarie, New South Wales (1821) This region beside the Hastings River replaced Newcastle as a penal settlement to isolate prisoners sent from the Port Jackson area. Following a decade of occupation, Port Macquarie was then converted into a place of exile for invalid convicts and 'Specials', a class of educated male convicts (such as actors, clerks, writers, artists) considered threats to law and order. Free settlement soon reached Port Macquarie and more distant stations were required.

Sarah Island, Macquarie Harbour, Van Diemen's Land (1821) The penal settlement was begun with male and female secondary offenders who worked at shipbuilding, naval trades, farming and timber-harvesting in this rich, yet

fig 11 *The Prisoners' Barracks at Moreton Bay followed the Georgian architectural formula found in many colonial buildings.*

remote, region in the Indian Ocean. After a decade of poor communications, escapes and alarms, Sarah Island closed in 1833. The remaining prisoners were transferred to Port Arthur. A brief reopening in 1846–47 was an ill-conceived experiment.

Moreton Bay, New South Wales (1824) An exploratory settlement at Redcliffe had many disadvantages and the following year, the garrison and male and female convicts moved up the Brisbane River to the present position of Brisbane, Queensland. This subtropical penal settlement closed in 1842 and free settlers moved in. Further shipments of convicts for assignment were received in the late 1840s. The Moreton Bay region was granted colony status in 1859.

Fort Dundas, Melville Island, Timor Sea (1824) This strategic settlement was established with convict labour to provide a British trade presence. The occupants soon found survival difficult in the tropics and Fort Dundas was abandoned in 1829.

Maria Island, Tasman Sea, Van Diemen's Land (1825) This isolated location to the north-east of Hobart was developed to receive incorrigible convicts as well as law-breaking colonials. The prisoners manufactured woollen cloth. Abandoned in 1832 but revived a decade later, the settlement was finally closed in 1850.

Port Arthur, Tasman Peninsula, Van Diemen's Land (1832) Port Arthur was opened as a place of secondary punishment for male convicts in an attempt to consolidate the widespread penal settlements in Van Diemen's Land. It became infamous. Some convicts were kept at work on ironwork, bronze-casting, shoe-making, pottery and other crafts while others were given hard labour. Although transportation to Van Diemen's Land was suspended in 1852, Port Arthur remained a penal settlement until 1877. The final occupants were Norfolk Island returnees, pensioners and transported felons whose sentences had not been completed.

Point Puer, Tasman Peninsula, Van Diemen's Land (1833) This prison for male juvenile transportees was an adjunct to the nearby Port Arthur penal settlement. It was intended to isolate the young offenders from the adult males. By 1842, there were 712 juvenile prisoners at Point Puer.[3] The site was closed in 1848.

Port Phillip Bay, Bass Strait, New South Wales (1837) Two early expeditions in 1803 (near Sorrento, Sullivans Bay) and 1827 (Corinella, Westernport Bay) failed in their attempts to establish settlements on Port Phillip Bay. Success came in the mid 1830s. In 1837, the Governor of New South Wales sent convict work gangs to perform public works in what was to become the free settlement of Melbourne. In 1841, convict numbers approached 240. The Home Office transported over 1,700 convicts directly to Port Phillip Bay from Britain between 1844 and 1849. Transportation in the Port Phillip colony ended in 1849–50 with a total of approximately 2,500 convict arrivals. Victoria became a separate colony in 1851.

The Swan River Colony, Western Australia (1850) Convicts were sent with a military detachment from New South Wales to King Georges Sound (Albany) in 1826 to establish a British presence in the western part of Australia following rumours of French interest in the area. However, the poverty-stricken Swan River Colony (Perth/Fremantle area), begun as a free settlement in 1829, petitioned the British Government to introduce convict labour in the late 1840s. The first convict transport arrived in 1850.

fig 12   *(previous pages) Beauty and cruelty were merged on the Tasman Peninsula when Port Arthur was established as a penal settlement.*

fig 13   *Convicts transported to Western Australia were met by some of the continent's most unusual landscapes.*

The arrival of transported convict labour helped solve the colony's chronic shortage of manual labour for public works and agriculture. In 1868, British transportation to Australia was suspended and the last convict ship arrived in Fremantle in October of that year. A total of 9,668 convicts was transported from Britain to Western Australia.

ENDNOTES

1   Alexander Solzhenitsyn, *The Gulag Archipelago*, Vols V–VII, Harper & Row, 1974–78, p.335.
2   *Historic Records of New South Wales*, Vol. 1, Part 2, p.142.
3   *Journal of Charles O'Hara Booth: Commandant of Port Arthur*, Tasmanian Historical Research Association, 1981, p.23, p.29.

4   *... [the women] will be furnished with employment*
in spinning flax, making straw hats or bonnets,
making up slops [work clothes] and other such work
as they may be capable of performing ...

FEMALE
FACTORY

Incarceration in the so-called Female Factories in Parramatta, Hobart, Moreton Bay and elsewhere was often the fate of transported convict women who found themselves in trouble with the colonial authorities. Women who aggressively resisted assignment as colonial servants were also sent to these places. Inside many of these walled compounds, described in the official returns as Female Factories, large numbers of women laboured to produce wool and linen yarn, fabrics, blankets, clothing, hats, bonnets, ropes, nets, stockings, needlework and other textile stores for the colony.

Equipped with some of the penal colonies' earliest industrial equipment such as spinning wheels, looms, fulling mill and stocking frames for knitting, some of the Female Factories in New South Wales, Queensland and Van Diemen's Land became Australia's first manufacturing concerns. The convict women, labouring under the piecework system refined in Europe's Industrial Revolution, were the colonies' first factory workers.

Although many of the Female Factories were in urban areas, the women were as socially isolated as their male counterparts in Macquarie Harbour or Port Arthur. Within these prisons, rebellious women were held in check

fig 14   *These Russian women aboard a convict barge took their place among the convict colonists of their nation's vast frontiers.*

by solitary confinement, restriction of rations, rock-breaking and the most resented punishment of all, hair-cropping. The Female Factories at Parramatta and Hobart were the scenes of tumultuous acts of defiance, violent riots and fires.

Despite the widespread colonial use of the term 'Female Factory', few of these compounds in rural areas produced trade items. A factory is usually defined as a building with facilities for the manufacture of goods. However, most of the womens' prisons in country areas were no more than holding areas for convict women awaiting assignment to an employer. Some served as 'lying-in' hospitals during childbirth or lockups for law-breaking females. This suggests that the term 'Female Factory', although widely used in correspondence, might have had an ironic meaning in colonial speech.

The use of female prisoners for textile factory labour has a long tradition in Europe. When John Howard, the noted prison reformer, wrote his book, *The State of the Prisons in England and Wales: With ...an Account of Some Foreign Prisons*[1], he observed that in Hamburg, Germany, the 'House of Correction' was a female workhouse: '... various kinds of work were carrying on; knitting, spinning, weaving linen, hair and wool...'[2] He also found Female Factories in the lowland cities of Amsterdam, Rotterdam, Delft and Ghent.

During the first years of the New South Wales penal colony, textiles were as scarce as rations. Any form of cloth was desperately needed for clothing. In 1801, the first Female Factory at Parramatta was processing wool and linen for weaving into cloth. By 1819, testimony before the Bigge Commission describes the male convicts' clothing in bounteous terms.

> *When each convict lands from the ship he receives: a suit of*
> *coarse woolen jacket and waistcoat of yellow and grey*
> *[ie unbleached] cloth, a pair of [cotton] duck trousers, a pair*
> *of worsted stockings, a pair of shoes, two cotton or linen*
> *shirts, a neck handkerchief, a woolen cap. [This ration is*
> *repeated every six months.]* [3]

The ration for repeat offenders at the Female Factory, Parramatta was similar:

> *Issue to Women of the Second Class [repeat offenders]*
> *...26 August 1824: one jacket made of blue gurran, one*

petticoat, one under petticoat of [Female] factory flannel,
two calico caps, two shifts, one neck handkerchief, one pair
of shoes.[4]

By the 1820s, the descriptions of convict clothing and blankets illustrate the economic importance of the products of the major Female Factories. In the *Sydney Gazette* throughout the months of April–August 1826, the retail price of Parramatta woollen cloth was as much as 2 shillings, 6 pence per yard compared to imported cotton muslin at prices of 2 shillings, 3 pence per yard to 3 shillings per yard.

THE FACTORIES AND THEIR WORK

The principal work of the Female Factories of New South Wales, Van Diemen's Land and the Moreton Bay settlement is summarised below.

The Old Parramatta Female Factory, New South Wales c1800–20 The Factory was originally built with a spinning loft, rope walks to fabricate cordage and factory rooms. By 1801, linen and wool were being processed.[5] In the following year, Governor King could report that 676 yards of blanketing, 279 yards of fine linen and 367 yards of coarse linen were processed.[6]

In 1804, nine looms [with male weavers] were employed weaving the Factory yarn. Blanketing, flannels and druggets were available by 1805.[7] By 1820, 158 women, 107 children, and 42 male convicts were employed here in textile manufacturing: washing, picking, carding, spinning, weaving wool [male weavers]; pulling, breaking, hackling, spinning, weaving linen; pulling, breaking, hackling, spinning hemp.[8]

The New Parramatta Female Factory, New South Wales 1821–48 In February 1821 the women moved into their new Parramatta factory where there were spaces for carding and weaving, loom rooms, a workshop, stores and a bleaching ground.[9] An 1822 inventory lists 44 spinning wheels, 26 wool cards and 114 pairs of worn-out wool cards.[10] The women also manufactured shoemaker's hemp, tow ropes and cheesecloth, among other products. Some of the tailors' shop duties were ultimately transferred to the new Factory facility from the Hyde Park Barracks where 26 male tailors were employed.[11] The Female Factory was also charged with making cushions for one of the colony's churches, as yet unidentified.[12]

By 1827, the supply of labourers and yarn allowed the Factory to weave 522 yards of cloth per week.[13] But despite this obvious success, weaving was discontinued in 1831 and the looms and related machinery were sold at auction.[14] Although weaving was suspended, the Factory's carding, spinning, tailoring and needlework were retained. Oakum picking (untwisting old cordage) was introduced for the most recalcitrant class of prisoners.

To supplement the role of the Female Factory, a government laundry was begun in 1837.[15] There was an attempt to develop a business in needlework on consignment, and rates for Female Factory sewing were advertised in the *Sydney Gazette* in the late 1830s and early 1840s:

> *[S]hirts from 1/o to 2/6 pence shifts 1/o -1/6 pence*
> *petticoats /6 -1/o pence slop clothing per suit 1/6 - 2/6*
> *pence All articles except tailor's work must be cut out ...*
> *[pick up and delivery at the Hyde Park Barracks.]*[16]

Finally, after the shutdown of the female convict transportation system, the Female Factory was closed, the equipment broken up and the building converted to a Lunatic and Invalid Establishment on 31 March 1848.[17]

Newcastle Female Factory, New South Wales c1818–48+ Although called a 'factory', the Newcastle Female Factory was never separate from the 1818 gaol. Although it was adjacent to the coastal salt works, there is no indication that prisoners from the gaol were ever employed there either. It appears that there was no meaningful work as the gaol was intended for refractory prisoners returned from assignment, or as a form of punishment for repeat offenders. A matron was appointed here in 1831 at a salary of 5 pounds per annum.[18]

The Moreton Bay Female Factory, New South Wales [Queensland] 1829–39 Women convicts were sent to Moreton Bay [Brisbane] as early as 1825. Erected in 1829, the Female Factory at the colony was enclosed by a high fence. The inner buildings had verandahs, a hipped roof structure, dormitory rooms, isolation cells, external kitchen, wash house and a matron's room.

In the Moreton Bay colony's 1829 regulations, it was noted that '... they [the women] will be furnished with employment in spinning flax, making straw hats or bonnets, making up slops [work clothes] and other such work as they may be capable of performing...'[19]

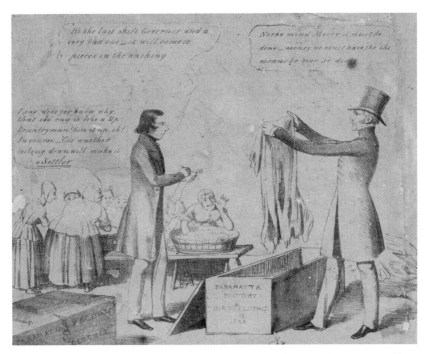

fig 15   *A government laundry was established at the Female Factory, Parramatta amid much public and private ridicule.*

James Backhouse's published account (1836) of his travels throughout Australia reports that the Female Factory work was washing, needlework, picking oakum and nursing in the Moreton Bay Hospital. The Factory closed on 27 May 1839.[20] In June 1839, Matron S Bell wrote to the Colonial Secretary asking what to do with 52 women and 16 children lately arrived. [21]

The Port Macquarie Female Factory, New South Wales c1831–42 This Factory, like Newcastle, was not used for labour. It was used for the confinement of pregnant women, and women awaiting assignment in the district. The presence of babies at the Factory is noted in the NSW Commissariat reports in 1834 on clothing issued to children at the Female Factory: 'newborn: a set of baby linen, all children above 6 mos. cotton bedgown, flannel petticoat, calico shift, cap, all supplied every six months'.[22]

In 1835, the Port Macquarie Female Factory reported 24 women and six children present. In 1839, 35 women and seven children can be found there.[23] Women were eagerly sought for assignment in the region. An 1838 letter from the Port Macquarie Police Office to Sydney describes the situation:

> *I have the honour to inform you that the total number of women in the Factory here is only fourteen, and amongst them there is not one assignable, they either being invalids or have young children. I therefore beg that from twelve to twenty female prisoners be sent here for assignment.*

The Bathurst Female Factory, New South Wales pre-1833–46 Despite its description as a Female Factory, Bathurst was an assignment depot. The women were kept in a separate building from the male prisoners; unassigned or repeat-offending women were sent to Parramatta. In 1838, Matron Sarah Keenan was earning a salary of 40 pounds/annum.[24] The 1839 returns show a listing of 42 women and 14 children in the Female Factory.[25]

Eagle Farm, Moreton Bay, New South Wales [Queensland] c1830–39 Women prisoners were employed sporadically at this agricultural site in the early 1830s. All women from the Brisbane Town Female Factory were transferred

fig 16   *These convicts are wearing parti-coloured uniforms similar to those manufactured at Parramatta and the Cascades.*

to Eagle Farm in 1837. By 1839, the site was closed down as free settlers began to move into this rich agricultural district.[26]

George Town Female Factory, Van Diemen's Land c1824–35 The George Town building, near Launceston, was originally constructed in 1821 as a parsonage. According to Tasmanian scholars, the Female Factory was formally begun in April 1823 and completed in 1824.[27] Professor MacKnight also notes that spinning and weaving took place there. Regulations state that First Class prisoners (the best-behaved) were to act as cooks, task workers and hospital attendants. The more recalcitrant Second Class women were to act as seamstresses. The so-called Crime Class was required to wash and process yarn.[28] In 1835, the George Town Female Factory was closed and the women sent to Launceston.[29]

The Launceston Female Factory, Van Diemen's Land 1834–46+ In December 1842, there were 227 women imprisoned in the Launceston Female Factory.[30] The women were employed in worksheds in the exercise yards of the radial prison. Their tasks included washing, needlework and spinning.[31] The *Hobart Town Gazette* reported on 29 December 1843, that washing could be done for 1 shilling and 6 pence per dozen articles.[32] At the 'Female House of Correction, Launceston' women were 'sentenced to the washtub' as a form of punishment.

Old Hobart Female Factory, Van Diemen's Land 1822–28 In 1816, there were only 75 assigned female servants in the colony of Van Diemen's Land and troublesome female prisoners were confined to a single room in the Hobart Gaol.[33] This arrangement proved unsuccessful and by 1818, refractory women were being sent to Parramatta in New South Wales. Labour was impossible in these conditions and in 1822, the government completed plans for a two-storey barracks directly beside the main Hobart Gaol, to house an estimated 100 female convicts.[34] This too, must have proved unsatisfactory and the nearby Cascades site was developed into the major Hobart Female Factory.

The Cascades Female Factory, Van Diemen's Land 1828–51+ This Factory was one of the womens' gaols that could be described as a significant manufactory. It was originally created from buildings of a distillery on the site outside of Hobart and extensive modifications made it one of Tasmania's most sophisticated industrial sites. The 1 January 1829 'Rules and Regulations for the Management of the House of Correction for Females' at Cascades clarifies their status:

> The dress of the females shall be of cheap and coarse materials and shall consist of a cotton or stuff gown, or petticoat, a jacket and apron with a common straw bonnet of strong texture ... 1st Class shall wear the dress without any distinguishing mark, 2nd Class by a large yellow C on the left sleeve of the jacket. 3rd Class with a large yellow C in the centre of the back of the jacket, one on the right sleeve and another on the back part of the petticoat.
> [Their labour was:] lst Class [work]: cooks, task workers, hospital attendants; 2nd Class [work]: making clothes, getting up linen; 3rd Class [work]: washing, carding wool, spinning ...[35]

In 1835, a blanket manufactory was added at the Cascades which required wider looms and the presence of a fulling mill to process wool-blanketing fabric within the textile complex.[36] The *Hobart Town Gazette* of 30 December 1843 reported 700 women at the Cascades with 102 sentenced to the washtub.[37] These women were accompanied by 29 children.

The Cascades textile manufactory continued to expand through the 1840s. New dyeing yards were constructed, new looms bought and reeling and winding rooms were added in 1843.[38] Public washing and plain needlework services at Cascades were advertised in the *Hobart Town Gazette* in the same year.

'... [T]here is a capital laundry and thousands of clothes are washed every month', reported C J LaTrobe in his 1847 report on Van Diemen's Land. 'The wool spun here is woven into blankets in a shop without [outside] the walls by paid pass holders ...' He also notes that most of the women had served probation on the *Anson* hulk where spinning was the primary activity on the vessel.[39] At the end of 1849, some 266 women at the Cascades continued to prepare wool fibre and yarn for manufacture of woollen cloth.[40]

fig 17   *The Female Factory at the Cascades outside of Hobart Town was the site of one of the most extensive manufactories.*

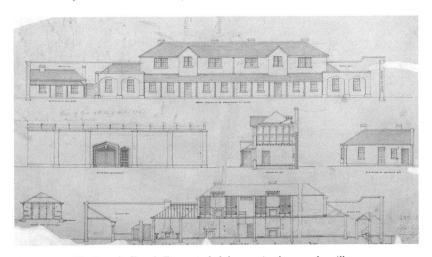

fig 18   *The Cascades Female Factory included a weaving house and ancillary rooms for textile production.*

Brickfields, Argyle Street, Hobart 1842–? This depot was originally constructed for male prisoners. In September 1841 it was closed and renovated as a labour depot for female prisoners acceptable for assignment. In the *Hobart Town Gazette* of 30 December 1842, it was advertised that there were 151 women at Brickfields available for assignment in the city or in the interior of Van Diemen's Land.[41] CJ LaTrobe's 1847 report on Van Diemen's Land noted that needlework was practised there.

Anson Hulk 1843–49 Although the *Anson* convict hulk anchored in the Derwent was never officially described as a Female Factory, many of the women kept on the hulk (fitted out by 18 October 1843) were kept active preparing and spinning yarn for the Cascades Female Factory.[42] The women made straw hats, bonnets and knitted stockings from the wool processed on board.[43] The *Anson* closed on 31 January 1849.

Ross Female Factory, Van Diemen's Land 1848–54 In May 1848 the old convict station at Ross was converted for use as a House of Correction for women, a female hiring depot and lying-in hospital for females.[44] It appears that little or no government work was performed there. The Ross site was closed in 1854 and given to the Catholic Church.[45]

ENDNOTES

1   John Howard, *The State of the Prisons in England and Wales with Preliminary Observations and an Account of some Foreign Prisons*, Warrington, London, 1778.
2   Howard, *The State of the Prisons in England and Wales*, p.116.
3   *Testimony of Major Druitt. J.T. Bigge Report*, Evidence, pp.36–42, Mitchell Library, State Library of New South Wales.
4   Colonial Secretary, *Regulations for Dress at the Female Factory at Parramatta*, 1824, Archives Office NSW [AONSW] 4/1708, reel 2802.
5   *Historic Records of Australia [HRA]* Series 1 Vol. 3, p.13.
6   *HRA* Series 1 Vol. 3, p.439, King to Portland.
7   *HRA* Series 1 Vol. 5, p.12, p.556.
8   JT Bigge, *Bonwick Transcripts*, Box 27, p.6616, SLNSW.
9   *HRA* Series 1 Vol. 10, p.690, Macquarie to Bathurst.
10   AONSW 4/1757, p.171c, Letters to the Colonial Secretary.
11   AONSW 4/3717, p.429, Macleay to Factory Committee.
12   AONSW 4/1783, p.125, Letters to the Colonial Secretary.
13   AONSW, 4/1957, Colonial Secretary, 1827.
14   *Sydney Gazette*, 11 October 1831, p.10.
15   AONSW 4/2359.1, Matron to Colonial Secretary, 37/8744.
16   *New South Wales Government Gazette*, Vol. 1, 25 March 1840.
17   AONSW 4/281, Colonial Secretary, Returns of the Colony, f.344, 1848.
18   AONSW 4/264, Colonial Secretary, Returns of Colony, fiche 2/, f.110.

19   *Regulations for Penal Settlements* [Moreton Bay] 1 July 1829, Governor Darling to Sir George
       Murray, HRA Series 1 Vol. 15, pp.104–1160.
20   AONSW 4/2451.3, Colonial Secretary re Female Factory 1839, 39/6041.
21   AONSW 4/2451.3, Colonial Secretary re Female Factory 1839, 39/60941.
22   AONSW 4/2234.5, Commissariat to Colonial Secretary FF 1834, 34/713.
23   AONSW 4/2492.1, Colonial Secretary re Female Factories 1840.
24   AONSW 4/270, Colonial Secretary, Returns of the Colony, fiche 2/4 f.214, 1838.
25   AONSW 4/2492.1, Colonial Secretary re Female Factory 1840.
26   P McLaren, *Eagle Farm: Former Agricultural Establishment, Female Factory and Prison*,
       Conservation Management Plan, Works Australia, Australian Estate Management 1996.
27   Campbell MacKnight, *University of Tasmania: Launceston* (personal communication),
       28 September 1997.
28   Laurel May Heath, *The Female Convict Factories of NSW and VDL: An Examination of their Role
       in the Control, Punishment and Reformation of Prisoners Between 1804 and 1854*, Master of Arts
       Thesis, ANU, 1978, p.177.
29   Heath, *The Female Convict Factories of NSW and VDL*, p.178.
30   *Hobart Town Gazette*, 30 December 1842, p.1129.
31   Heath, *The Female Convict Factories of NSW and VDL*, p.230.
32   *Hobart Town Gazette*, 29 December 1843, p.1391.
33   *Statistical Account of Tasmania from 1804 to 1823*, Hobart, 3 December 1856, p.7, quoted in
       Heath, *The Female Convict Factories of NSW and VDL*, p.162.
34   *HRA*, Series 1 Vol. 10, p.700, Macquarie to Bathurst, 27 July 1822.
35   Colonial Secretary's Office 1 January 1829, reprinted in Philip Tardif, *Notorious Strumpets and
       Dangerous Girls*, Angus & Robertson, 1990, Appendix 4.
36   Heath, *The Female Convict Factories of NSW and VDL*, p.169.
37   *Hobart Town Gazette*, 30 December 1843, p.1129.
38   Heath, *The Female Convict Factories of NSW and VDL*, pp.217–218.
39   CJ La Trobe's Report is reprinted in Ian Brand, *The Convict Probation System: Van Diemen's Land
       1839–1854*, Blubber Head Press, 1990, pp.201–202.
40   Heath, *The Female Convict Factories of NSW and VDL*, p.226.
41   *Hobart Town Gazette*, 30 December 1842, p.1129.
42   Archives Office of Tasmania, CSO 22/102/2164, p.47.
43   Heath, *The Female Convict Factories of NSW and VDL*, p.206.
44   Heath, *The Female Convict Factories of NSW and VDL*, p.234.
45   *Ross Female Factory*, Parks and Wildlife Service Tasmania, n.d.

5   *'How much is each Labourer's daily task?'*
     'Seven Rods [of hoeing]. It was eight, but on their
     representing to the Governor that it was beyond their
     strength to execute, he took off one.'

NATION
BUILDING

In the past decade, a radical reassessment of the convict system has toppled the gothic image of the illiterate and ill-trained convict man and woman. Painstaking analyses of British and colonial records show that the labour skills and literacy levels of transported convict men and women were equal, or in many cases superior, to the equivalent working populations in England and Ireland. These findings were originally assembled in *Convict Workers*, edited by Stephen Nicholas.[1] This original work has been amplified by authors such as Deborah Oxley in *Convict Maids*.[2]

The information for many of these reassessments comes from British record-keeping. Before embarkation for transportation, convict indents often recorded each prisoner's personal details such as occupation, age, literacy, stature, physical appearance and other matters. On debarkation in Australia, similar examinations took place. On close study, these documents reveal convicts with a wide range of valuable skills. In New South Wales, the urban skills of tailors, tanners, blacksmiths, bakers and bootmakers dominated over rural skills such as farming, shearing and fieldwork.[3] Most convict women fell into the category of domestic servants. Oxley reports over 50 per cent in her sample.[4]

fig 19   *A photograph from the 1927 convict film, 'For the Term of His Natural Life',*
           illustrates a 19th century reality: men as beasts of burden.

Naturally, the government was anxious to extract as much value as possible from this human capital and there were few nation-building tasks not undertaken by individual convicts and convict gangs. However, convicts were also employed as members of the convict establishment: constables, gaolers, floggers and overseers.

In general, male and female convict labour was employed by the military Governors of the colonies in the following ways:

- Through government assignment of individuals to private masters;
- The formation of government gangs and workshops to labour on specific tasks or projects such as shoe-making, tailoring, bridge and road-building, and furniture-making;
- Through the issue of Tickets of Leave documents that left convicts free to work and profit from their labour, but the individual still remained a convict subject to recall or restrictions. They had to remain in their districts and attend convict musters;
- A Conditional Pardon which allowed liberty for the former prisoner subject to selected conditions (ie. not to return to England). These convicts were generally free to work as they wished;
- An Absolute Pardon allowed individuals (emancipists) the freedom to labour as they wished. They also had the immediate right to return to Britain. A convict having served his or her sentence was described as Free by Servitude (after seven or 14 years) and classified as Expirees. They, too, could return to their homeland if they chose.

WORKING THE 'GOVERNMENT STROKE'

This slang expression was used in the convict era to describe the labour performed by prisoners for the colonial government. The following excerpts were chosen to give a sample of the broad range of activities carried out by convicts and a sense of the forces that affected transported men and women at labour.

The Hours of Work (1825) 'The working hours are to be from sun-rise till sun-set, allowing one hour for dinner; and, during summer, to those out of doors, one hour for rest, from eight till nine o'clock in the morning...'[5]

fig 20   *The Ross Bridge, Ross, Tasmania, was designed and constructed by convict labour. It features many carved portraits.*

Status among Convict Workers (1821) [Mr Hutchinson, Superintendent of the Hyde Park Barracks before the Bigge Commission]. 'What employment do you conceive to be the most severe ?' 'That of lime-burning, quarrymen, blacksmiths, bullock drivers, woodcutters, sawyers and carters.'

[What of the] The Town Gang [?] 'Generally the most inefficient men. They are employed in loading and unloading the government colonial vessels at the dockyard wharf.'

[What of] The Jail Gang [?]. '[They are employed] ... clearing away the rubbish from the quarries, loading and unloading vessels from the Coal River, sometimes digging foundations. They all work double-ironed upon a single ration in a party coloured [parti-coloured] dress.'[6]

Convict Labour in Western Australia (1850–62) '... 563 miles of road cleared, made and repaired; 167 miles of road drained ... 6,600 yards of stone causeway were made and 7½ miles of earth embankment, 239 bridges erected or extensively repaired and 12,900 yards of approaches to bridges ... 4,000 trees felled and removed from roads...44 wells sunk, 14½ miles of tramway laid, 2,260 yards of fencing prepared and fixed; two jetties and a sea wall...'[7]

Brickmakers (1793) 'The account which I received from the brickmakers of their labours was as follows. Wheeler ... was tasked to make and burn ready for use 30,000 tiles and bricks per month. He had 21 hands to assist him, who performed everything; cut wood, dug clay, etc.'[8]

Road Building in New South Wales (1829) 'The Road to the Southward ... is opened to the extent of 150 miles and 253 Men are employed on it at present. The Western road to Bathurst also occupies a space of 120 miles from Emu Plans, on which 320 men are now employed. On the Road to Hunter's River by Wiseman's on the Hawkesbury, which is not yet completely opened, nearly 400 men are employed...' Governor Darling to Sir George Murray, 20 August 1829.[9]

At the Forge in Hobart Town (1847) '[The] Forge, Hobart Town. 7 Mechanics. Carpenters making sashes for Ferrymens' hut at Bridgewater, and hand-cart wheels; Smiths completing anchor for punt at Rest Downs, and steeling stone hammers.'[10]

Agriculture and Hoeing (1793) [Parramatta] 'The plough has never been tried here; all the ground is hoed and very incompetently turned up. Each convict labourer was obliged to hoe sixteen rods a day (approximately 80 metres), so that in some places the ground was but just scratched over.'[11]

[Government gang, three miles north of Parramatta] 'How much is each labourer's daily task?' 'Seven rods [35 metres of hoeing]. It was eight, but on their representing to the governor that it was beyond their strength to execute, he took off one.'[12]

Sewing and Tailoring (1798) 'The employment of the male convicts here [Sydney] ... was the public labour. Of the women, the majority were compelled to make shirts, trousers and other necessary parts of dress for the men, from materials delivered to them from the stores, into which they returned every Saturday night the produce of their labour.'[13]

Convicts Workers in the Port Phillip Colony (1839–40) '... between 70 and 80... [convict workers]' Lonsdale to Colonial Secretary, 27 July 1839.[14] '...prisoners in the service of the government amounting to over

180 persons...' Superintendent, Port Phillip, January 1840.[15]

The Tailors Gang (1825) 'Every tailor is tasked with making two suits of slop clothing daily; the cloth used for this purpose is made at the Female Factory, Parramatta. All the watchmen's greatcoats are made in this shop at the rate of one daily per person.'[16]

Convict Workshops at Port Arthur (1830–50) Bookbinders, carpenters, tinsmiths, shoe-makers, blacksmiths (casting and forging), wheelwrights, wood and metal turners, potters, tailors, brickmakers and shipbuilders.

Tanning of Leather (1822) [Mr Wilshire, tanner, before the Bigge Commission.] 'Do you supply the Military here with leather?' 'Yes, I do. I have

fig 21   *This relief from the Ross Bridge is considered a portrait of Lieutenant Governor George Arthur.*

Seen the shoes served out to them from England, and they are of a very inferior quality to those made up from the leather purchased here. Instances are common of [the Military] Selling their shoes ... and taking [my] leather.'[17]

Shoe-making (1821) [Mr Hutchinson, Superintendent of the Hyde Park Barracks before the Bigge Commission.] 'How many shoemakers are employed in the [government] lumberyard?' 'About 14 or 15. Each workman makes a pair of strong shoes per day.'[18]

Public Buildings Constructed with Convict Labour in Perth, WA Colonial Hospital (1855), Perth Boys' School (1854), Court House and Gaol (1856), Residence and Office for Dean of Perth (1859), Government House (1864), Pensioner's Barracks (1863), Perth Town Hall (1867). Convict transportation ceased in 1868.[19]

Shipbuilding, Macquarie Harbour, Van Diemen's Land (1824–27) From 1824 to 1827, the convict-operated shipyard on Sarah Island, Macquarie Harbour, built the brig *Derwent*, two sloops, the schooner *Governor Sorell*, a 16-oared launch, a lighter, gigs, whaleboats, longboats, dinghies and twelve smaller craft for a total of 35 vessels. Macquarie Harbour was abandoned in 1833.[20]

Major Druitt's Description of the Trades practised in the Government Lumber Yard, Sydney (1819) '... Carpenters, Joiners, Cabinet makers, Wood turners, ... wheelwrights ... Smiths for all sorts of country work, Tool makers ... Iron and Brass Founders ... turners and platers, Iron and brass wire drawers ... Tinmen, Painters and Glaziers, Farriers and horse shoers ... Taylors, and shoemakers, Gunsmiths, File makers and cutters, Comb makers, Block makers, Coopers and Millwrights, Machine makers, Anchor smiths.'[21]

Major Government Lumberyards in the Penal Colonies The Newcastle Lumber Yard; The King's Yard, Hobart Town (mark: KY); Parramatta Lumber Yard (mark: PY); Port Macquarie, New South Wales; Sydney Lumber Yard (mark: SY); Port Arthur (mark: PA); smaller yards at Norfolk Island, Sarah Island, Macquarie Harbour, Van Diemen's Land and Moreton Bay.

Brooms at the Hyde Park Barracks (1841) The Select Committee on Security of Life and Property questions Captain H H Brown, of the Hyde Park Barracks:

fig 22 (*previous pages*) *This appears to be a rare illustration of a convict indent (Bermuda) where the prisoners' histories are taken and their skills assessed.*

'Are you aware of the practice of sending out [convict] men every day in gangs to collect material for making brooms?' 'Yes.' 'Do you think all these brooms are necessary for the [convict] establishment in Hyde Park?' 'No.' 'Do you think the men sell brooms [to the public]?' 'I am sure they do. If you were to watch the wood cart from the time it leaves the Canterbury Bush, you will find that it was filled by five or six feet. By the time it arrived at the barracks it would be level with the cart; the men sell it as they go along.'[22]

ENDNOTES

1   Stephen Nicholas (ed.), *Convict Workers: Reinterpreting Australia's Past*, Cambridge University Press, Cambridge, 1988.
2   Deborah Oxley, *Convict Maids*, Cambridge University Press, Cambridge, 1996.
3   Nicholas, *Convict Workers*, p.68.
4   Oxley, *Convict Maids*, p.119.
5   *Instructions for the Guidance of the Superintendent and Subordinate Officers of the Establishment of Convicts in Hyde Park Barracks*, Government Printer, Sydney, 1825, p.4.
6   *Bigge Report*, Interview with William Hutchinson, Principal Superintendent of Convicts, 24 January 1821, Mitchell Library, 39804/179.
7   Selection from 'The Amount of Work Performed by Convict Labour ... June 1850 to November 30, 1862', Royal Engineers Office, Western Australia, 1862, in Julie Ball, *A Preliminary Study of Convict Sites in Western Australia*, Fremantle Prison, 1997.
8   Watkin Tench, *A Narrative of the Expedition to Botany Bay and A Complete Account of the Settlement at Port Jackson*, [1789, 1793] Tim Flannery (ed.), Text Publishing Company, 1996, p.152.
9   *Historic Records of Australia*, Series 1, Vol. 15, p.125.
10 'A Return of the Distribution of Convicts in Van Diemen's Land ... for the Week ending the 2nd of January, 1847', reprinted in Ian Brand, *The Convict Probation System: Van Diemen's Land 1839–1854*, Blubber Head Press, Hobart, 1990.
11 Tench, *A Narrative of the Expedition to Botany Bay*, p.154.
12 Tench, *A Narrative of the Expedition to Botany Bay*, p.215.
13 Tench, *A Narrative of the Expedition to Botany Bay*, p.226.
14 NSW Colonial Secretary Letters Received, AONSW 4/2471, 39/021.
15 Superintendent Port Phillip, Inwards Correspondence, Series 19, 40/83, Asst. Colonial Surgeon to La Trobe 29 January 1840, in Martin Sullivan, *Class and Society in the Port Phillip District*, PhD. Dissertation, Monash University, July 1978.
16 Major Horton to Colonial Secretary, (1825) *Historical Records of Australia*, Series I, Vol. XI, p.650.
17 *Bigge Report*, Interview with James Wilshire, tanner, 23 January 1822. John Ritchie (ed.), *The Evidence to the Bigge Reports*, Heinemann, 1971, p.114.
18 *Bigge Report*, Interview with William Hutchinson.
19 Julia Ball, *A Preliminary Study of Convict Sites in Western Australia*, Fremantle Prison, 1997.
20 Richard Davey, *Sarah Island: The Penal Settlement*, Tasmanian Parks and Wildlife Service, n.d.
21 Ritchie, *The Evidence to the Bigge Reports*, p.21.
22 *Report of the Select Committee on Security of Life and Property* [in Sydney], Charles Nicholson, Chair, Sydney, 1841, p.54.

...when a Regiment embarks for Garrison Duty
on foreign service, the lawful wives of the soldiers
shall be permitted to embark, in the proportion
of Twelve per Company...

IN THE
LOGS

Like so many other international penal colonies, Australia was ruled by a procession of military Governors. Appointed from the Navy and the Army, these officers also administered military justice until the provision for a civil judiciary in the early 19th century.

The officers and enlisted men of the British Marines (1788–91) from the First Fleet of convict transports, then British Army troops (1790–1870) provided governance, enforced public order and oversaw the internal and external security of the colony. By 1870, when British regiments were no longer posted to Australia, over 30 British Army Regiments and other units had served in the colony.

While some law-breaking soldiers and sailors took up the unexpected role of convict, other members of the military were encouraged to settle in the colonies with the offer of grants of land and government concessions in establishing businesses. It was possible at various times for discharged soldier/settlers to receive tools, livestock and rations from the government stores for themselves and their families. Discharged enlisted men's allotments were modest and rarely exceeded 300 acres.[1]

fig 23   *Hair-cutting and shaving was a form of ritual humiliation for men and women.*
French prisoners queue for the convict barbers.

However, Colonel Erskine of the 48th Northhamptonshire Regiment (in Australia from 1817–25), received a grant of 3,000 acres in August 1818, a sizeable parcel of land now known as Erskine Park.² Major Druitt, also of the 48th Regiment, the 'Chief Engineer of the Convict Establishment' took up 1,000 acres in the Rooty Hill district not long after Erskine assumed ownership of his generous parcel.

Many army officers and enlisted men entered the economic world of the new colony with enthusiasm. A number of the officers in the early regiments used their international contacts and lines of credit to import goods for speculative sale. The New South Wales Corp (in Australia from 1790 to 1810) became extensively involved in the trade in spirits. The 48th Regiment ran its own flour mill and bakery (established by earlier regiments) and sold processed flour and bread to the New South Wales Government Commissary.³

Military families made up a high percentage of the free population in the first decades of the settlement. Wives and children were able to travel with their husbands' regiments. The women and children who 'Followed

fig 24   *One of the British soldier's most persistent foes in the convict colony of New South Wales was boredom.*

the Drum' provided Australia with some of its first free settlers. The British Army Regulations stated:

> ...when a Regiment embarks for Garrison Duty on foreign service, the lawful wives of the soldiers shall be permitted to embark, in the proportion of Twelve per Company, [ten companies per regiment] including the wives of Non-commissioned Officers, and Rations are to be issued to them as long as the Corps remains in a Foreign Garrison.[4]

If there were more than 12 married families with the Company, the women and children were chosen by a ballot arranged by the Company's pay sergeant. The convention of children among the British Army serving in the colonies was so well-established that after 1811, a Regimental Schoolmaster was gazetted. School was often provided for girls as well as boys.[5]

The Army's central role in designing and constructing the civic centres of the new colony was as important as its place in the colony's society. As the Army was the advance party for most of New South Wales' secondary settlements such as Norfolk Island, Newcastle, Hobart Town and Moreton Bay, military commanders and their engineers initiated rudimentary town planning and erected civic buildings. Captain Wallis, the commanding officer of a detachment of the 46th Regiment (in Australia 1814–19) at Newcastle, for example, was responsible for much of the early development of the town including the design and construction of Christ Church, Newcastle.[6] All of Australia's capital cities, except Darwin, were set out by British military officers.

In New South Wales, Major George Druitt of the 48th Regiment, as the Chief Engineer of the so-called Colonial Establishment, was responsible for the colony's public works and buildings during the appointment of the convict Francis Greenway as the Government Architect. Without Druitt's coordination of artisans and materials, Greenway's great civic commissions would have been impossible. Major Druitt was also responsible for the Government Lumber Yard, in Sydney, a strategic centre for the artisans and supplies necessary to build and maintain a colonial outpost.

Captain (later Lieutenant Colonel) George Barney, of the Royal Engineers (posted to Sydney 1835–44), also played a major role in shaping New South Wales with his construction of Sydney's Circular Quay, his plans for the Fort Denison and Bradley's Head fortifications as well as maritime improvements throughout the colony. During his tour in Australia, Barney was elected President of the School of Arts, a bank trustee and the Chair of the Gaslight Company.

Supervised convict labour was essential for public works. During convict transportation in the eastern colonies, the Army was often directed to supervise iron gangs for country road-building, oversee their labour on government building projects, design and direct the log construction of rural gaols (the origin of the expression 'in the logs') and other building and engineering tasks. The rigorous discipline of the Army allowed the troops to carry out difficult roles in some of the colony's most remote areas.

The colonial military government also supervised the judicial system and administered punishments to the convicts. Military juries in courts lingered until 1839 with a Judge Advocate (an appointed civilian) and six military officers acting as jury.[7] Army officers were also appointed as magistrates in remote settlements but were restricted in the punishments they could impose on convicts. Army punishments could be much more severe than those dealt out to prisoners. This discrepancy between the 'scenic punishments' of flogging for soldier and convict must have been a constant source of friction for these antagonists.

The relations between the convicts under sentence and the colony's numerous military garrisons have scarcely been studied. A survey of revolts of five or more prisoners demonstrates that well-trained, disciplined troops were necessary to maintain colonial order. When large-scale rebellions occurred among convicts, the Army was needed to restore order. Incidents were frequent. Although Australia was an isolated island prison, colonial records reveal that the possibility of escape was never far from the prisoners' minds. Groups of convict men and women attacked their keepers, stole ships, torched their gaols and 'bolted' to the bush.

A small selection of group (five or more convicts) revolts and rebellions from 1791 to 1846 follows:[8]

1791	9 April. Mutiny aboard the transport *Albermarle*. Two convicts hanged.
1793	25 May. Mutiny planned aboard the transport *Sugar Cane*. Attempt foiled.
1795	12 September. Mutiny aboard the transport *Marquis Cornwallis*. Forty-two men flogged.
1797	1 August. Mutiny aboard the transport *Lady Shore*. Male and female convicts and their military escort escape to South America.
1798	11 March. Attempted mutiny aboard the transport *Barwell*. Attempt foiled.
1800	16 November. Convicts seize the government sloop *Norfolk*.
1801	29 December. Convict mutiny aboard the transport *Hercules*. Fourteen executed.
1804	5 March. Insurrection involving 200 or more convicts in the Hills District outside of Parramatta is defeated by a military detachment. Eight convicts hanged.
1808	16 May. The brig *Harington* seized by convicts at Farm Cove. Convicts escape to the Philippines.
1813	23 April. Convicts seize the government schooner *Unity* in Van Diemen's Land.
1816	16 September. Convicts seize the government boat *Trial*.
1817	25 July. Convicts seize the government boat *William Cossar*.
1820	28 February. Convicts attempt to seize the transport *Castle Forbes* in Van Diemen's Land. The plan fails and 14 arrested.
1823	7 May. Convict mutiny aboard the transport *Ocean*.
1826	10 December. Convict mutiny aboard the brig *Wellington* off Norfolk Island. Boat retaken.
1827	October. Riot and mass escape at Female Factory, Parramatta, after selected rations are taken away.
1829	12 July. Convict rebellion aboard the transport *City of Edinburgh* bound for Moreton Bay from Sydney. Six convicts wounded.

1829	14 August. The government boat *Cyprus* seized off Macquarie Harbour, Van Diemen's Land. Convicts sail to Japan.
1831	4 February. Riot and escape at Female Factory, Parramatta. Female overseer seized and her head shaved by convict women.
1834	11 January. The government brig *Frederick* seized by convicts at Macquarie Harbour. Convicts escape to Chile.
1834	15 January. Conspiracy on Norfolk Island. Nine convicts killed by soldiers during rebellion and 13 other prisoners hanged following trials.
1835	16 October. Convicts seize William Charles Wentworth's sloop *Alice*. Boat found beached north of Port Stephens.
1842	21 June. Convicts attempt to seize the government brig *Governor Phillip* while unloading at Norfolk Island. Five convicts killed, four convicts executed.
1843	17 February. Over 100 female convicts riot in Female Factory, Parramatta. Windows and doors broken. Chief Constable injured.
1846	1 July. 'Cooking Pot Riot' on Norfolk Island after convicts' cooking utensils are seized by Commandant. Three constables and overseer killed. Twelve convicts executed.

As the colony of New South Wales continued to expand, the military force that could be marshalled by a traditional garrison of foot soldiers was dissipated by distance. In the mid-1820s, the colonial administration in New South Wales asked that a group of mounted soldiers be assembled to combat bushrangers active in the Bathurst and Hunter Valley regions. These troops could be moved rapidly.

Once approved by Britain's Secretary of State for the Colonies, a troop of 'light cavalry' was raised to police the rural areas in New South Wales. The soldiers, selected for their fitness and martial abilities, were picked from the serving regiment in the colonies. As the Mounted Police, they served as the rural police force until 1850, a civilian police force was then recruited to serve in the country regions. By 1839, the largest units of the Mounted Police were based in Goulburn, Bathurst and Maitland, New South Wales.[9]

The relative successes of the Mounted Police in New South Wales

fig 25   *The formation of the Aboriginal Police in the Port Phillip settlement was celebrated by the artist William Strutt.*

encouraged an adaptation of additional Mounted Police units in the southern colony. In the Port Phillip settlement, a severe shortage of labour and troops led the Army Commander to recruit, outfit and train units of Aboriginal Australians into a uniformed 'Black Police'. The unit was used to supplement the mounted troopers in their campaigns for law and order.

Captain William Lonsdale (4th Regiment, in Australia 1832–37), in his role as Magistrate and Superintendent, expressed grave concerns about runaway convicts from Van Diemen's Land and elsewhere.[10] Lonsdale could only assemble a small military force: the District Constable and two Deputy Constables in the new colony. A trained Aboriginal troop could supplement their modest numbers.

Aborigines had been asked to help track down convict escapees from the first appearance of the European colonists and convicts in the 18th century. This long-standing practice must have aggravated early racial tension between Aboriginal Australians and the convicts.

In May 1837, Captain Lonsdale requested the formation of a mounted police unit for the new settlement[11] and by September 1837 the Colonial

Secretary Edward Deas Thomson had approved the scheme. In October, 15 Aborigines had joined, and received blankets, clothes and a daily ration. Based at Dandenong, they promised their European leaders to 'give up native habits'. Chronic military mismanagement caused this first unit of Aboriginal police to disband.

The 'Black Police' detachment was revived in 1842.[12] This time, Captain Henry Dana was their Commanding Officer. He recruited some 23 troopers and their unit ultimately achieved a strength of 65 soldiers. A total of 140 Aboriginal troopers served in the group. The 'Black Police' was finally dissolved in 1852.

There were other regional attempts to establish 'Black Police' detachments. In 1837, the British intellectual Alexander Maconochie drew up plans for an Aboriginal police force in Tasmania which were presented to Governor Bourke.[13] Maconochie also wished to recruit an Aboriginal regiment. But his entreaty was cut short by Governor Bourke who responded that he had already authorised Captain Lonsdale to employ them in the Port Phillip constabulary.[14]

In Western Australia, Aboriginal Australians were also assigned in 1841 to police detachments at Perth, Guildford, Fremantle, and Albany. All had been discharged by 1845.[15] In 1864, the position of Aboriginal Police Assistant was revived in Western Australia but only ostlering and tracking were allowed.[16] The historian Henry Reynolds reports that Aboriginal forces were established in northern New South Wales by 1848.[17] Queensland took over the supervision of these units by 1859 and the 'Black Police' role in the new colony continued until the 20th century.[18]

The military was an inseparable part of the structure of the Australian penal colony from 1788 to 1870. In addition to providing for the public order by supplementing the civilian police, the soldiers' and sailors' role in the service, in the judiciary, the colony's economic life, the early creation of schools, in city planning, building and intellectual activity was essential to Australia's successes as well as its failures. Many soldiers and sailors who chose to remain in the colony acquired property and established families that made major contributions to the former penal colony's transition from isolated outpost to regional centre.

ENDNOTES

1   Clem Sargent, 'The New South Wales Garrison 1788–1842', *Historic Houses Trust of New South Wales Report*, 1997, p.26.
2   Sargent, 'The New South Wales Garrison', p.13.
3   Clem Sargent, *The Colonial Garrison 1817–1824*, TCS Publications, 1996, p.27.
4   *British Army Regulations and Orders 1816*, p.370, facsimile in Sargent, 'The New South Wales Garrison', Appendix, p.18.
5   Sargent, 'The New South Wales Garrison', Appendix, p.19.
6   Sargent, *The Colonial Garrison*, p.11.
7   Paula-Jane Byrne, *Criminal Law and Colonial Subject*, Cambridge University Press, 1993, p.12 and Juries Act, (1839), 3 Vict. No.11, s2.
8   'Convict Revolts and Rebellions', Report compiled by Beverley Earnshaw for the Hyde Park Barracks Museum, Historic Houses Trust of NSW, 1997.
9   Sargent, 'The New South Wales Garrison', Appendix, p.35.
10   Marie Fels, *Good Men and True: Aboriginal Police of the Port Phillip District 1837–53*, Melbourne University Press, 1988, pp.7–10.
11   Fels, *Good Men and True*, p.10.
12   Les Blake, *Captain Dana and the Native Police*, Neptune Press, 1982, pp.15–16. (See also Henry Reynolds, *With the White People*, Penguin, Melbourne, 1990, p.49, citing La Trobe to Colonial Secretary. Enclosed Gipps to Stanley 21/3/1844. Dispatches from Governor of NSW, Vol. 44, 1844.
13   Reynolds, *With the White People*, p.47.
14   Reynolds, *With the White People*, p.49.
15   Neville Green, *The Forrest River Massacre*, Fremantle Arts Centre Press, 1995, p.63.
16   Green, *The Forrest River Massacre*, p.63.
17   Reynolds, *With the White People*, p.49.
18   Reynolds, *With the White People*, pp.50-51.

7   *... [N]ative-born families prove essentially conventional:*
     they played with toys and games invented by their parents,
     they attended school, they learned trades. They formed
     communities and ultimately, they became us.

FAMILY

'...I have by a regular line of good conduct & great privations arrived at a state of comfort...', wrote the convict Sarah Thornton to her British family in 1820.[1] Sarah had been transported for theft, arriving in Sydney in 1814. Sarah's 'comfort' came from her children (at least five) and her tailor husband, who was a free settler.[2] Their massed economic and social power allowed Sarah's family to navigate the straitened circumstances of a convict colony.

Sarah Thornton's opportunities were rare. The First Fleet arrived in Botany Bay in 1788 with a convict cargo of 552 men and 190 women. This unbalanced ratio of male to female became a chronic problem for Britain's colonial administrators. By the second quarter of the 19th century, Britain grew anxious for the colonies to develop a society along more conventional lines. This was a difficult task in a land where a balanced male and female population did not appear until 1921.[3]

The gender imbalance meant that the colonial population's liaisons were often unconventional. The records reveal that homosexuality was not uncommon among men and women. Many who entered into heterosexual

fig 26   *This watercolour detail of the Newitt family was painted by the twice-*
            transported convict Charles Costantini.

relationships ignored the ritual of formal matrimony. With English and Irish spouses far away, married soldiers, settlers and convicts openly practised de facto bigamy.

In the first three decades of settlement, a considerable percentage of Catholic convicts were deprived of the sacrament of marriage as there were no Catholic priests in New South Wales and Van Diemen's Land until 1820–21. Until the Colonial Marriage Act of 1834, only Anglican marriages were legally valid.

Under fierce pressure from the Governors and the colonies' religious leaders, prisoners were offered incentives to marry. In order for convicts or settlers to progress socially or economically, matrimony could be an advantage. The institution of the traditional British family and the matrimonial vows of the Church of England provided the first colonial models.

Unlike the situation in Britain, the New South Wales Governors provided centralised assistance for modest education and training for colonial children in orphanages, schools and apprentice systems. The first Female Orphan School was opened in 1801. Five years later, there were six similar institutions. The children of the first generation of convicts formed a significant percentage of the second generation of Europeans in Australia. The lives of Australian-born children were essentially conventional: they played with toys and games invented by their parents, they attended school, they learned trades. They formed communities and ultimately, they became us.

The story of Susannah Watson (1794–1877), who arrived in 1828, gives an insight into the forces that helped and hindered the formation of convict families during the transportation era. Fortunately, Susannah's life has been traced in rigorous detail by Babette Smith in her 1988 book *A Cargo of Women: Susannah Watson and the Convicts of the Princess Royal*.[4]

Watson was born in 1794 in London into a labourer's family. Her father worked at a trade and was identified as literate. In 1817, Susannah married Edward Watson. They had seven children, of whom five survived. Susannah became a chronic thief and she was transported for 14 years with her nursing baby Thomas Watson (d 1831) aboard the ship *Princess Royal*. Susannah's convict records in Sydney note her literacy and professed skills as a needlewoman and a housemaid.

fig 27   *Very few games, toys and other material evidence of convict family life have survived. Toys, in particular, seem ephemeral.*

When Susannah, separated from her husband and most of her children, arrived in Sydney in May 1828, she was assigned to a shipwright's Australian-born family in The Rocks area. Convicts on assignment could form de facto relationships but they could not formally marry without the government's approval. If a petition to marry was opposed by the convict's employer, it had little chance of acceptance. In 1828, men made up about 76 per cent of the colony's population.[5]

In 1830, at the age of 36, Susannah Watson became pregnant to Isaac Moss and gave birth to a boy Charles, at the Parramatta Female Factory. The Factory served as a centre for textile production, a prison, a hiring depot as well as a nursery. Convict women who became pregnant without the protection of a conventional relationship were sent to the Female Factory for their 'lying-in' period.

Children were reared at the Parramatta Factory until the age of three, when they were taken from their mothers and placed in Orphan Schools. The government cart called twice a year to collect the children. When Orphan School boys turned 10, they were placed in trade apprenticeships.

By the mid-1830s, formal apprenticeships for males bound the trainee until age 21. Girls remained at the Orphan School until they married or found domestic work.

By 1831, Susannah had been assigned to a freed convict family in Parramatta, but she was soon arrested for stealing and received a two-year sentence. She was returned to the Female Factory. Convict men and women on assignment to families or individuals were required to work each day and to be 'regular' in their habits. Absenteeism was discouraged and employers could return their assigned convicts if they proved troublesome. Susannah's assignment was lost because of her crime.

During 1832, after a remitted sentence for theft, Susannah Watson formed a de facto relationship with convict John Clarke (husband II). In 1834, at the age of 40, she gave birth to a son John Henry, at the Parramatta Female Factory. In the following year (1835), her son Charles was sent from the Female Factory to the Orphan School, Liverpool. In order to maintain their de facto status, John Clarke managed to have Susannah Watson assigned to him. The government assignment of convicts to de facto spouses was an unorthodox but practical method of encouraging the stability of convict families.

Unfortunately, John Clarke was sentenced to an Iron Gang for theft in 1836. This left Susannah Watson briefly on her own and eligible for reassignment. Their daughter Agnes (d 1842) was born the following year and John was able to have his sentence suspended. This allowed the family to re-form. In 1838, John Clarke petitioned for the release of Susannah's son Charles from Orphan School.

Before Susannah could travel to Liverpool to pick up her son, she was returned to the Female Factory by her new assigned Parramatta employers and was unable to obtain reassignment. She was trapped within the Factory until she could be reassigned and regain custody of her children. To complicate matters, Susannah's de facto husband reoffended and received another Iron Gang sentence. He vanished from Susannah Watson's life.

In 1839, when he was five, Susannah's son John Henry left the Female Factory nursery (two years behind schedule) and was sent to the Orphan School at Liverpool. But in 1840 Susannah Watson received a Ticket of

Leave allowing her to reside in Parramatta. This permitted her to collect John Henry from the Orphan School and for the first time in several years, Susannah and her three surviving Australian-born children, John Henry, Charles and Agnes, were reunited.

However, the same year, Susannah stole again and her Ticket of Leave was suspended. It is not known where her children were kept during the time she served her sentence. In 1841, she left the Female Factory and her daughter Agnes died the following year.

In 1843, Susannah, 49 and still burdened with her convict status, married the gardener William Woollard (husband III) in a Protestant service. William was a former convict transported for life. Although government approval was given for the marriage, she was technically a bigamist, since her husband, Edward Watson, was still alive in Britain. The following year, Susannah was granted a Certificate of Freedom. Although the era of convict transportation officially ended in 1840, Susannah carried a 14-year sentence. She served it all.

The desire for marriage was strong despite the unevenly matched male and female population. At the time of Susannah Watson's marriage to William Woollard, the percentage of males in the colonial population was approximately 64 per cent. This meant that despite her age, Susannah's domestic skills and good health insured that she remained a valuable marriage partner. After six years of marriage, Woollard died, leaving her in the care of her two sons, John and Charles, who were now of working age.

Two years later, in 1851, Susannah, then 57, married John Jones (husband IV). John Jones died in 1856 and Susannah again came under the dependent care of her surviving sons in Braidwood in 1857. In 1859, Susannah re-established contact through the post with her surviving family in Britain. Susannah Watson died at the age of 83 in Boulder Hill, near Gunning, New South Wales in 1877.

Babette Smith's detailed biography confirms Watson's near-instinctual desire to form families. Families meant comfort, a physical and mental ease, satisfaction and contentment. By combining the strength, wit and abilities of partners and children, new strengths could be realised. For example, by her alliance with John Clarke, Susannah Watson could obtain the release of

her child Charles from the Liverpool Orphan School. The status of family also lent convicts a moral authority otherwise unattainable.

The Church of England's Book of Common Prayer is explicit on the ideas of comfort and the social capital to be gained from marriage. From the 'Solemnisation of Matrimony':

> *[Matrimony] was ordained for the procreation of*
> *children ...*
> *[Matrimony] ... was ordained for a remedy against sin,*
> *and to avoid fornication ...*
> *[Matrimony] ... was ordained for the mutual society, help*
> *and comfort, that the one ought to have of the other,*
> *both in prosperity and adversity.*[6]

The 'mutual society' of the family also meant enhanced economic bargaining power. Children could work with their parents in their trades, shops or services. A stable family could also receive permission to change residence to pursue work while a convict without family might be rejected. Freed convicts, of course, needed no such permission.

Alan Atkinson points out that convict women overwhelmingly sought to marry free or Ticket of Leave men. These liaisons made the women effectively free.[7] Very few convict women chose to marry convict men on assignment or in government custody.

Marriage could also help one obtain land. Government land grants were available for convicts who had served their sentences and wished to settle. However, a conventional 30-acre land grant could be increased to 50 acres for a formally married convict and the presence of children could mean as much as a grant of 10 additional acres per child. Generally, the granting of Tickets of Leave could also allow married convict couples to purchase land.[8]

While offering encouragement in some respects, the government could also offend against the institution of the family. Transportation itself was a disruptive act that shattered families for a generation or more. The practice of removing children from the age of three from their convict mothers to the Orphan Schools was equally damaging. It established a precedent for legal seizure and separation of children that continued into the late 20th century.

But despite the forces that worked against the formation of convict families in the penal colonies of New South Wales, Van Diemen's Land and the Swan River colony, ardent de facto and formal relationships were established, children were created and families were formed. Recent works such as Grace Karskens's *The Rocks: Life in Early Sydney*[9] and Alan Atkinson's study *Camden: Farm and Village Life in early New South Wales*[10] reveal the constancy, even the normality, of family life within the villages and towns.

The power and endurance of the three convict family lines featured within the exhibition – the Joseph Slater (b1816) and Sarah Stowell (b1820) family from New South Wales; the James Roe (b1818) and Susanne Moore (b1818) family from Western Australia; and the William Henshaw (b1828) and Elizabeth Brodie (b1822) family from Tasmania – illustrate their unquenchable desire for domestic comforts that leads directly to the present generation of these families.

ENDNOTES

1   Tom Sear's 'Research Report on Convict Familial Relations', 1999 for the Hyde Park Barracks Museum stresses the importance of 'comfort' in forming family units.
2   Patricia Clarke and Dale Spender (eds.), *Life Lines*, Allen & Unwin, 1992, p.138 for full text.
3   See gender population figures in Wray Vlampew, *Australians: Historical Statistics*, Fairfax, Syme & Weldon Associates, 1988.
4   Babette Smith, *A Cargo of Women: Susannah Watson and the Convicts of the Princess Royal*, University of New South Wales Press, 1988.
5   Interpolated from Vramplew.
6   *The Book of Common Prayer*, George Eyre and William Spottiswoode, London, 1859.
7   Alan Atkinson, 'Convicts and Courtship', *Families in Colonial Australia*, P Grimshaw, et al., (eds.), Allen & Unwin, 1985.
8   Atkinson, 'Convicts and Courtship', p.23.
9   Grace Karskens, *The Rocks: Life in Early Sydney*, Melbourne University Press, 1997.
10 Alan Atkinson, *Camden: Farm and Village Life in early New South Wales*, Oxford University Press, 1988.

8   *The handling of food and drink was subject to*
     wholesale abuse and the cooks and stores supervisors
     were always suspect. Some of the most violent
     convict rebellions resulted from food disputes.

ON THE
STORES

Convicts labouring within the government system were 'on the stores'. Their rations and clothing came through the government supply system. Convicts 'off the stores' could be on assignment and their employers responsible for their food and clothing. Prisoners might be on a Ticket of Leave and required to support themselves. Men and women 'off the stores' had an opportunity to discard the characteristic linen or wool uniforms worn by convict workers in favour of conventional colonial attire. They could eat food of their own choosing. The freedom to eat, drink and dress as one pleases is not to be underestimated.

Until transported convicts could obtain the leisure and means to cultivate their own crops or sell or barter their labour to purchase their own food, the government stores issued the 'pease, pork and porridge'. Within the penal colony system in New South Wales, the Commissary was responsible for the purchase, storage, transport and issue of rations, forage, quarters and other physical requirements. The Commissary also issued supplies to the convicts, the military and other members of the population who found themselves 'on the stores' (such as superintendents, overseers, magistrates, pensioners and others).

fig 29   *For convicts everywhere, food was a source of constant friction. It was a*
            medium for rewards as well as punishments.

From 1788, the Commissariat reported to the Colonial Governor but after 1809, the Colonial Commissary General was appointed by the Commissary General in England.[1] The Commissariat administrators held military rank but had no command responsibilities. They might obtain stores from Britain, purchase goods within the colonies or acquire supplies offshore. The entrepreneurial 48th Regiment (in Australia 1817–25), supplied vegetables, flour and bread through its own mill and bakery for the New South Wales Commissary. The 48th Regiment also held the Commissary's vegetable concession for the Hyde Park Barracks.[2] Other regiments were granted similar concessions. Rations were the source of continual dispute among the convicts. The handling of food and drink was subject to wholesale abuse and the cooks and stores supervisors were always suspect. Some of the most violent convict rebellions were the result of food disputes. Food preferences among convicts and others were also conservative. They sampled indigenous cuisine only during severe shortages. Archaeologists have demonstrated that many convicts preferred to eat salt pork and salt beef from government stores rather than fresh kangaroo or other Australian mammals.[3] This phenomenon can be verified by comparison of colonial newspaper prices for salted meats compared to kangaroo. Salt meat was avidly sought.

While the image of starvation and short rations surrounds convict life, Stephen Nicholas and other authorities have calculated that prisoners' regulation diets when converted to kilojoules (calories) often exceeded the 20th century minimum daily requirements set for young, mature males.[4] However, the distribution of food could be unreliable as well as inequitable; the restriction of rations was also used as a form of punishment. These problems unquestionably affected nutrition and health.

GOVERNMENT RATIONS

An abbreviated survey of government regulations for food suggests some of the variety and quantities of convict rations:

- In the week of 20 June 1806 in New South Wales. 'To all Males; 4½ lb salt pork, or 8 lb beef. 4 lb flour or 5 lb wheat or, 5½ lb barley or 6 lb maize. 6 oz sugar.'[5]

- 20 May 1811 in New South Wales. 'Settlers, Freemen and Prisoners. Salt beef 7 lb and pork 4 lb., Wheat 6 lb., Maize 15 lb.[weekly].'[6]
- 24 September 1823 in New South Wales. 'Scale of Weekly rations. Parramatta [Female] Factory. 3½ lb fresh meat, 7 lb wheaten flour, $\frac{1}{16}$th sugar, 2$\frac{1}{16}$th tea. [Child's Rations, above 7 years] 3½ lb fresh meat, 7 lb flour.'[7]
- 29 June 1831, New South Wales Government Order. The weekly rations for assigned convicts are 'twelve pounds of wheat or nine pounds of flour or in lieu [of the above], three and one-half pounds of maize meal and seven pounds of flour, seven pounds of beef or mutton, or four and one-half pounds of salt pork, [and] two ounces of salt'.
- 24 July 1837. Juvenile Establishment, Point Puer [Van Diemen's Land]. '...Dinner at half past twelve. This meal consists of ¾ lb Fresh, or Salt Beef, or ½ lb Salt Pork, 10 ounces Pudding, made from 7 oz of flour, with the Fat procured from boiling the Meat... [per Boy].'[8]
- On 1 July 1845, 'The Daily Ration for the... [Female Convicts of Van Diemen's Land]. ⅚ lb. of 12 per. cent. Flour, or 1 lb. of Bread. ½ lb. of Meat. ½ lb. of Vegetables. ½ oz. of Salt. ¼ Pint of Oatmeal.'[9]

There was considerable barter value in these stores from the government Commissariat. The chronic shortage of currency and coinage, and the convict's lack of access to it, ensured that government-issue rations and clothing had real economic worth. The vast number and types of bones in the Hyde Park Barracks archaeology collection reveals that convicts consistently concealed meat and bones inside and outside the building. Perhaps they recycled bones into useful objects such as gaming pieces, accessories and handicraft for sale or trade. Their food rations, edible or inedible, were a medium of exchange.

Concealing, stealing or misappropriating food and clothing could constitute an offence so these activities usually took place in secret. If caught, a convict was punished by loss of privileges, flogging or a sentence to the government treadmill.

In the Australian setting, the treadmill was used as a human-powered engine to drive mill wheels for grinding grain into flour. In a 19th century

fig 30   *These convicts on the treadmill in Burma could easily supply enough power to grind grain or pump water.*

penal colony where labour was scarce and technical achievement was modest, utility was important. The British treadmill, described by English convicts as an apparatus for 'grinding air', was transformed into a valuable colonial milling machine for grinding grain.

There were two treadmills operating at the Carters' Barracks, Sydney, on the site of Central Station, in 1825. The larger mill was adapted for male offenders only and 36 prisoners could go 'on the steps' working in short shifts. The New South Wales Committee on Tread-Wheel Labour report (1825) notes that the diameter of Sydney's largest wheel at the Carters' Barracks was 18 feet, 8 inches (approximately 5.6 metres) in circumference and rotated twice a minute. Both devices powered grain mills.

There was a treadmill and granary complex at Port Macquarie, New South Wales, and a hand-turned crank mill at Norfolk Island. A treadmill-powered flour mill was in operation at Moreton Bay [Queensland] at the site of the government windmill; wind-power and convict-power were used alternatively. The windmill site survives in downtown Brisbane.

Treadmills were also in use in Hobart Town, Van Diemen's Land, in the 1830s. By the 1840s, the new settlement of Port Phillip [Victoria] had its own treadmill. In 1847, a treadmill was in operation at Port Arthur [Tasmania] that utilised 36 men. The diameter of this wheel was 35 feet (over ten metres). The Port Arthur flour mills relied on three sets of millstones; two of them were operated by water power.[10]

Food was so central to human existence that it proved a continual cause for disruption and punishment. As the thieves from the 'Three Penny Opera' sing, 'Food is the first thing, morals follow on'.[11] The first convict to be executed in New South Wales, Thomas Barret, was hanged on 28 February 1788 for plundering the colony's meagre stores. Barret was the first European put to death in Australia by the British.

In the following year, six Royal Marines accompanying the First Fleet were hanged by the colony's Public Executioner for plundering the Commissariat stores in March 1789.[12]

Some of the penal colonies' major convict rebellions were also provoked by food. On 27 October 1827, a riot broke out in the Parramatta Female Factory when the rations of sugar, bread and tea were suspended. A large number of female convicts managed to breech the wall and escape from the Factory. On 31 October, the *Sydney Gazette* wrote that '...the inmates of the Factory were quickly poured forth, thick as bees from a hive...'

In 1846, the infamous penal settlement on Norfolk Island was the location of another bloody revolt over food privileges that cost 16 lives. On 1 July, the new Commandant of Norfolk Island, Major Joseph Childs, in an attempt to tighten discipline among the convicts, revoked their cooking privileges and seized the prisoners' government-issued cooking pots. The result of this interference with food rituals was a spontaneous rebellion that saw three constables and an overseer killed and 12 convicts executed by hanging.

In the colonial penal system, convict rebellions were continuous, but in the British military regime, iron discipline insured that mutinies were rare. However, rations were also a major issue for British soldiers and sailors and the revolt of elements of the 80th Regiment (in Australia 1836–44) at Norfolk

Island demonstrated just how important food could be to the troops.

The 50th Regiment (in Australia 1834–41) based at Norfolk Island had a tradition of cultivating gardens through allotments of land. These allotments were elaborately worked and some garden plots had huts built on them. When the 50th Regiment was relieved by a detachment of the 80th Regiment, the departing soldiers sold their gardens to the relieving men.

The 80th detachment's commanding officer, Major Thomas Bunbury, disliked the troopers' gardens and soon ordered a working party of convicts to destroy them. The convict work gang was driven off by the soldier-gardeners. Major Bunbury's response was to send a military detachment to destroy them; but the Major was met with a mutiny of 40–50 armed soldiers of his own regiment. The result was stalemate.

Major Bunbury and his detachment were recalled to Sydney and replaced with another unit. Eight of the gardener mutineers were court-martialled and seven were sentenced to Transportation for Life and one was transported for seven years. Major Bunbury received a severe reprimand.[13]

Norfolk Island also provides a final point of reference for violence associated with rations. In January 1854, the three-year-old Victorian colonial government appointed John Price as Inspector-General of Penal Establishments overseeing the five prison hulks anchored in Hobson's Bay, off Williamstown, Port Phillip Bay [Victoria]. John Price was the former Civil Commandant of the more than 2,000 convicts of Norfolk Island (1846–53). On Norfolk Island, food deprivation was one of Price's tactics for obtaining obedience during his seven-year command.

The Port Phillip colony had been receiving British convicts throughout the late 1840s and its five prison hulks and inland stockades and gaols were crowded. When Price took over the Victorian prison system, there were 1,056 offenders under the system.[14] Many of the prisoners were employed on public works.

On 26 March 1857, when a minor revolt occurred among an 88-man Williamstown work gang over alleged short bread rations, John Price confronted the convicts. After his party rejected most of their food complaints, the convicts suddenly attacked. While the overseers fled, Price fought but was knocked down by a stone, then seized by several of the prisoners and

fig 31   *The mid-day meal ('tiffin') for the transported Indian convicts at the*
            Andaman Islands penal settlement.

battered to death with stones, fists and a shovel. The bloody aftermath of
this fight over bread was a trial of 15 convicts and a Victorian record for
hanging eight men in a week.[15] Within the convict system, prisoners were
willing to die for food.

There were also deadly conflicts over rations between Aborigines, European convicts and colonists. Henry Reynolds and other observers have noted
the intense competition for food and land on the fringes of settlement.[16]
The Aborigines were immediately faced with two problems. First, the
European farming and hunting practices soon began to decimate their regional food sources. The almost immediate clearing of land in the Sydney
basin for construction materials resulted in major changes in plant ecology.
Indigenous animals were driven further into the bush.[17]

Reynolds also identifies the adaptation of European rations into the
Aboriginal diet as an significant culinary disturbance. This includes European
wheat flour, mutton, beef, sweet potatoes and even tea. When competition for
scarce food resources and land radically altered hunting and food-gathering
practices, Aboriginal Australians could also find themselves 'on the stores'.[18]

fig 33   *Aboriginal Australians and the Europeans soon found themselves in competition for fish and game.*

This offered the colonial government a tool to manipulate Aboriginal groups. Rations could be a reward for cooperation.

A few excerpts from the literature of the convict period illustrate the tensions over food between Aborigines and Europeans:

> *When fish are scarce, which frequently happens, [the Aborigines]…often watch the moment of our hauling the seine [net], and have more than once been known to plunder its contents, in spite of the opposition of those on the spot to guard it; and this even after having received a part of what had been caught.*[19]
>
> – WATKIN TENCH, ARMY OFFICER, 1788

> *[A] pleasure party…last week…made an excursion to Newcastle. Provided with excellent dogs, the kangaroo afforded a pleasant and profitable sport. One of the creatures, closely pursued, coursed to the water side;*

and despairing of escape, at length plunged in.[20]

– Sᴠᴅɴᴇʏ Gᴀᴢᴇᴛᴛᴇ, 1807

*When prevented by tempestuous weather or any other
cause, from fishing, these [Aboriginal] people suffer
severely. They have then no resource but to pick up
shellfish, which may happen to cling to the rocks and be cast
on the beach, to hunt particular reptiles and small animals,
which are scarce, to dig fern root in the swamps or to
gather a few berries...*[21]

– Wᴀᴛᴋɪɴ Tᴇɴᴄʜ, Aʀᴍʏ Oꜰꜰɪᴄᴇʀ, 1788

*[1830] In the neighbourhood of Sydney, the Natives are
growing scarce; the Whites locating so much land has
destroyed their hunting grounds and means of subsistence,
but still occasional groups are seen wandering through the
streets, vending fish, flowers or other trifling matters, for
the purpose of procuring grog ...*[22]

– Aᴜɢᴜsᴛᴜs Eᴀʀʟᴇ, 1830

And in conclusion, some observers of convict food:

*The pork had been salted between three and four years
[ago], and every grain of rice was a moving body from the
inhabitants lodged within...Our usual method of cooking
...[the pork] was to cut off the daily morsel and toast it on
a fork before the fire catching the drops which fell on a slice
of bread...*[23]

– Wᴀᴛᴋɪɴ Tᴇɴᴄʜ, Aʀᴍʏ Oꜰꜰɪᴄᴇʀ, 1788

*One male convict was executed [for stealing from the
stores]; one female convict and one child died [during the
1790 rationing]. The female convict occasioned her own
death, by overloading her stomach with flour and greens,
of which she made a mess during the day, and ate
heartily; but, not being satisfied, she rose in the night
and finished it. This was one of the evil effects of the
reduced ration.*[24]

– Dᴀᴠɪᴅ Cᴏʟʟɪɴs, Mᴀʀɪɴᴇ Oꜰꜰɪᴄᴇʀ, 1790

*For the first time I went fishing for giant oysters. You fish
for them at the end of the bay with a long-toothed iron
rake. This rake has a handle about 12 to 13 feet long and
you rake the bottom of the water with this rake and ...
withdraw ... [it] ... carefully ... A dozen of these oysters are
enough to satisfy an ordinary person.*[25]

     – Francois-Maurice Lepailleur, Convict, 1841

*Our fare [at Norfolk Island] was excessively meagre; at
breakfast and supper we ate insipid hominy ... nominally
sweetened with an ounce of sugar per diem, really about
half that quantity. A morsel of salt junk [meat], very like
old saddle, was served out for dinner, and nauseous, coarse,
maize bread, tasting as if it were composed of sawdust.*[26]

     – JF Morlock, Convict, 1844

*[The rations supplied to the convicts were] ... hominy for
breakfast ... one pound of brown bread, and half a pound of
animal food: this formed the daily allowance to each person,
if I might except the liquor termed soup, in which the fresh
meat is boiled, with a slight sprinkling of cabbage leaf.*[27]

     – Charles Cozens, Convict, 1840

*By secretly crushing fresh beef bones, we collected from
the surface of the water, made to boil with heated stones,
in a wooden vessel, a relish far more wholesome than bad
[government] butter.*[28]

     – JF Mortlock, Convict, 1844

You don't starve, but you are always hungry.[29]

     – Francois-Maurice Lepailleur, Convict, 1840

ENDNOTES

1   Clem Sargent, 'The New South Wales Garrison', 1788–1842, Historic Houses Trust of NSW, 1997, Appendix, p.5.

2   Clem Sargent, *The Colonial Garrison*, 1817–1824, TCS Publications, 1996, p.27.

3   Dominic Steele, 'An Historical Assessment of Convict Diet in Sydney 1788–1840', Historic Houses Trust of NSW, 1997, pp.12–14.

4   Stephen Nicholas, 'Care and Feeding of Convicts', *Convict Workers: Reinterpreting Australia's Past*, Stephen Nicholas, (ed.), Cambridge University Press, 1988, pp.180–198.

5   Steele, 'An Historical Assessment of Convict Diet in Sydney 1788-1840', Appendix 2, pp.54–68.

6   Steele, 'An Historical Assessment of Convict Diet in Sydney 1788-1840', Appendix 2, pp.54–68.

7   Steele, 'An Historical Assessment of Convict Diet in Sydney 1788-1840', Appendix 2, pp.54–68.

8   Captain Charles O'Hara Booth to Lt Governor, V.D.L. Tasmanian State Archives, CS05/35/728 in *Handbook for the Point Puer Database*, Robin McLachlan, (ed.), Mitchell College of Advanced Education, 1985.

9   Regulations of the Probationary Establishment for Female Convicts in Van Diemen's Land, 1 July 1845, in Ian Brand, *The Convict Probation System: Van Diemen's Land 1839–1854*, Blubber Head Press, 1990.

10   LaTrobe Report of 1847 reprinted in Brand, *The Convict Probation System*, 1990.

11   Bertholt Brecht and Kurt Weill, 'What keeps Mankind Alive', in *The Three Penny Opera*, 1928.

12   Watkin Tench, *A Narrative of the Expedition to Botany Bay and A Complete Account of the Settlement at Port Jackson* [1787–91], Tim Flannery, (ed.), Text Publishing Company, 1996, p.102.

13   Sargent, 'The New South Wales Garrison', p.38.

14   JV Barry, *The Life and Death of John Price*, Melbourne University Press, 1964, p.72.

15   Barry, *The Life and Death of John Price*, pp.106–107.

16   See Henry Reynolds, *The Other Side of the Frontier*, Penguin, 1982.

17   Reynolds, *The Other Side of the Frontier*, pp.111–113. AW Crosby, *Ecological Imperialism*, Cambridge University Press, 1986, provides an international context for this issue.

18   See James Kohen's discussion of the dramatic dietary changes in 'Contemporary Aboriginal Societies' in James Kohen, *Aboriginal Environmental Impacts*, University of NSW Press, 1995.

19   Tench, *A Narrative of the Expedition to Botany Bay*, p.53.

20   *Sydney Gazette*, 23 August 1807.

21   Tench, *A Narrative of the Expedition to Botany Bay*, p.260.

22   Augustus Earle, *Views in New South Wales and Van Diemen's Land: Australian Scrap Book*, J Cross, London, 1830.

23   Tench, *A Narrative of the Expedition to Botany Bay*, p.123.

24   David Collins, *Account of the English Colony in New South Wales, 1789–1802*, AH & AW Reed, 1975, p.89.

25   Francois-Maurice Lepailleur, *Land of a Thousand Sorrows*, University of British Columbia Press, 1980, p.89.

26   JF Mortlock, *Experiences of a Convict*, GA Wilkes & AG Mitchell (eds.), Sydney University Press, 1965, p.65.

27   Charles Cozens, *Adventures of a Guardsman*, Richard Bentley, London, 1848, pp.117–118.

28   Mortlock, *Experiences of a Convict*, p.82.

29   Lepailleur, *Land of a Thousand Sorrows*, p.12.

9   *...our well grounded anxieties on this question,*
    for the safety and happiness of all we hold dear upon
    this earth, cannot, and will not subside until
    transportation to any part of Australia be abolished
    at once and for ever...

GILDED
INIQUITY

Convict transportation had many opponents in Britain as well as in the colonies. After convict transportation from the British Isles was suspended in New South Wales in 1840, attempts by the British Colonial Office to reinstate the practice in Sydney, the Port Phillip Colony [Victoria], and Moreton Bay [Queensland], led to widespread social unrest. During this interlude, transportation continued until 1853 to Van Diemen's Land [Tasmania] and Norfolk Island until 1846. The most effective Australian opposition to the revival of this practice was led by the Australasian Anti-Transportation League. The organisation had active chapters in all the capital cities except the Swan River Colony. In Western Australia, the free colonists considered convict transportation essential for their economic success.

When the Anti-Transportation League was founded in 1849, it focused and legitimised the colonial struggle. The League met newly arrived convict ships with mass demonstrations, charismatic leadership and splendid oratory in Sydney and Melbourne. The British Government eventually lost its will and withdrew its plans. Transportation was finally terminated in Van Diemen's Land in 1853 (the last convict ship arrived on 26 May) and abandoned in

fig 34   *The end of convict transportation to Van Diemen's Land was commemorated*
           by rapturous celebrations.

Western Australia in 1868. Over 160,000 convict men, women and children were transported to the Australian colonies from 1788 to 1868.

Before the 1840s, convict transportation had been consistently criticised as immoral, uneconomical and counterproductive as a deterrent to crime. Public opposition in Britain finally led to the appointment of a Select Committee of the House of Commons on Transportation on 7 April 1837. The Committee, led by Sir William Molesworth, released its report on 24 November 1837: 'Transportation, though chiefly dreaded as exile, undoubtedly is much more than exile; it is slavery as well; and the condition of the convict slave is frequently a miserable one...'[1]

The Committee recommended that the present system of transportation of convicts to New South Wales and settled areas of Van Diemen's Land be abolished.[2] Norfolk Island and Port Arthur in Van Diemen's Land were to be reserved for banishment for long-sentence prisoners and chronic offenders.

While some historians suggest that some of the decisions regarding transportation had been made in the British Cabinet before the Molesworth Committee released its report, the government announced an end to transportation to New South Wales in October 1840. Convict exile was to continue to Van Diemen's Land and Norfolk Island. The convict transport *Eden* was the last official ship to New South Wales, arriving on 18 November 1840.

Some colonial landowners and agriculturalists suffered from the loss of free convict labour and they soon found a champion in William Charles Wentworth, a powerful member of the New South Wales Legislative Council. Wentworth, born on Norfolk Island to a convict mother, was willing to be identified with the revival of convict transportation in his 1843 election on a ticket with Dr William Bland, who had been transported for duelling. The truculent election crowds in Sydney jeered Wentworth calling him 'Norfolk Islander' and 'The Duke of the Lash and the Triangle'.

By 1846, the imminent suspension of transportation to Norfolk Island and Van Diemen's Land had also been announced. However, convict transports continued to quietly disembark on both islands. Seeking to enlarge the flow of prisoners, the British Secretary of State, WE Gladstone, made a formal query to the New South Wales Colonial Governor, Sir Charles Fitzroy, regarding the revival of transportation to New South Wales. William Charles Wentworth and his allies in the Legislative Council appointed a 'Select Committee' on 13 October 1846 to study Gladstone's proposal.

Within a fortnight, on 22 October 1846, Sydney's City Theatre was the site of a mass protest against Gladstone's request. But despite the public outcry, the Legislative Council's preliminary 'Report of the Select Committee on the Revival of Transportation', tabled 31 October 1846, recommended the revival of convict transportation.

The Committee requested no less than 5,000 male convicts per year and asked that the numbers of new convicts and assisted immigrants be equalised. It also noted that some 40,000 women were needed in the colony. Following the release of this report, the *Sydney Morning Herald* of 31 October 1846 editorialised that '…As leagues are rather fashionable just now, might not an "Anti-transportation League" be formed with advantage?'. It proved a timely suggestion.

Within a year of the Legislative Council's report, an 'Order in Council' on 4 September 1847 from the British Government ordered the renewal of convict transportation to Van Diemen's Land and New South Wales. In the same month, the New South Wales Legislative Council's Select Committee on the Revival of Transportation tabled its final report. The Wentworth Committee's recommendations for renewal, and Earl Grey's 'Order in Council', were defiantly rejected by the Colony's Legislative Council.

Some critics of transportation had compared the evils of slavery with the use of convict labour. Wentworth's Committee unintentionally verified their analogy by a callous computation of the cash value of a transported convict: 'The approximate cost, per head, of the transportation of a British Convict to Australia … £30 per convict (exclusive of maintenance)'.[3] For comparison, in 1848, the cost of a slave in Brazil was £45–50; in 1850 in St Louis, Senegal, a male slave cost £28.[4]

In Van Diemen's Land, the pace of convict transportation was accelerated in 1848. Secretary of State for the Colonies Earl Grey wrote to the Van Diemen's Land Lieutenant-Governor Sir WT Denison explaining that transportation would be revived in a slightly different form.[5] The British

fig 35   *A commemorative medallion was coined by the Royal Mint, London in honour of the rebirth of Van Diemen's Land as 'Tasmania'.*

Government's new convict transportation policy was now a period of confinement in Britain, then employment on public works, followed by exile to Australia.

On 24 January 1849, one of the first formal anti-transportation groups met in Launceston and vowed that it would not hire a convict who arrived in the colony after 1 January 1849. It was supported in its goals by John West, the Minister of the Congregationalist Church, Launceston. This was the beginning of John West's lengthy campaign against convict transportation. His extensive collection of news cuttings on the transportation debates is in the Hyde Park Barracks exhibition on loan from the Mitchell Library.

Convict ships were also arriving at the Port Phillip colony. On 15 November 1844, the *Royal George* anchored in Port Phillip with over 20 Pentonville Prison 'exiles'. The *Thomas Arbuthnot* arrived on 4 May 1847 with 288 'exiles'. (The 'exiles' were pardoned convicts from Pentonville, Millbank and Parkhurst prisons who had 'agreed' to immigrate.)

By 6 March 1849, the anti-transportation unrest spread to Port Phillip (independence from New South Wales came in 1851) and a mass meeting passed several resolutions. Among them were warnings that there was public alarm at the intent to make Port Phillip a penal settlement; that transportation was ruinous to this new colony and that the public was willing to physically resist landing convicts. A deputation from the meeting was appointed to wait upon Lieutenant-Governor LaTrobe.[6]

Shortly afterward on 15 May 1849, the New South Wales Legislative Council 'Respectfully Declined' the renewal of convict transportation. The motion was put by the anti-transportation leader Mr Charles Cowper:

> *[the] ... Legislative Council ... declines to accede to the*
> *proposal ... for the renewal of Transportation to this colony*
> *and strongly protests against the adoption of any measure*
> *by which the colony would be degraded into a penal*
> *settlement.*[7]

By unfortunate coincidence, the convict transport *Hashemy* anchored in Sydney Cove on 11 June 1849 and 5,000 citizens gathered at Circular Quay for a spirited protest meeting. The gathering was addressed by three New South Wales leaders: Robert Campbell, John Lamb and Robert Lowe. Despite the furore, some of the 239 convicts disembarked and coastal vessels sailed for Moreton Bay with 59 remaining prisoners.

Despite the colony's antipathy to convicts, random shipments of prisoners continued to arrive. For example, on 8 August 1849, the convict transport *Randolph* laden with 'exiles' and transported convicts sailed into Port Phillip Bay. Lieutenant-Governor C J LaTrobe ordered the Master of the vessel to sail on. The *Randolph*'s convicts landed in Sydney.

In April 1850, Earl Grey defiantly announced that Her Majesty's Government would now resume full-fledged transportation to New South Wales and Van Diemen's Land. Earl Grey's news provoked a September rally against convict transportation that drew 6,000 people to Barracks Square, Sydney. Encouraged by this public support, the Legislative Council resolution on 1 October 1850 called upon the British Government to revoke their earlier 'Order in Council' for the renewal of convict transportation.

The British Government's tenacity produced a Melbourne public meeting on 1 February 1851 which established that new colony's first official anti-transportation organisation. A Van Diemen's Land delegation also attended and the joint meeting swore not to hire transportees, to 'refuse fellowship' to those who aid or hire transportees, and to keep the League alive as long as there was transportation. 'The constitution of the League is to secure by moral means only, the Abolition of Transportation to the Australasian colonies. All who sign the League and Solemn Engagement [are] to be members.'[8]

This joint meeting was also the first appearance of the Australasian Anti-Transportation League's flag. 'A conference was held on the 1st of February 1851 at the Queens Theatre, where the Van Diemonians Delegates attended, who brought over with them a League Banner to be unfurled on the occasion.' 'The Banner of the League was next unfurled amidst three hearty cheers. It was of blue ground, with the stripes and cross of the National Union, and the addition of four stars on the ground work.'[9]

An even larger Anti-Transportation League conference took place in Hobart Town in 20 April – 12 May 1852. It drew delegations from Melbourne, Geelong, Launceston, Hobart Town, Midland and Sydney. The conference resolved that a petition 'embodying all the resolutions of the Legislative Assemblies in the several colonies on this subject should be prepared and ... land before the British Parliament and Her Majesty the Queen'. The mood of the speakers, as reported by *The Empire*, Sydney, 1 July 1852, was now dangerously revolutionary:

Mr James Norton. 'The revolution that must be wrought by the people of Australia must be by mild measures, by people deeply affected in the welfare of their country and in the future prospects of the rising generation.'

Mr Holden, supporting the conference resolution. '...[H]owever far rebellious thoughts might be from the mind, yet repeated injuries would but too surely excite men to strike.'

Mr GA Lloyd. '[A] ... spirit of discontent ... had been excited by the mismanagement of the colonies [and] if that mismanagement continues, would increase till it resulted in a rupture with the mother country. (Cheers.).'

Mr Gilbert Wright, supporting the Resolution. 'Now that they had become Australia Felix they should cease to be Australia Supplex. (Hear, Hear.) If their wrongs remained un-redressed, they should imitate the example of their Brethren of the United States. (Hear, Hear.)'

fig 36   *A ceremonial arch was raised In Launceston, Tasmania when the cessation of convict transportation was announced.*

The Conference's resolutions were accepted and passed to the Governor-General.

Despite the civil unrest, the Colonial Office remained adamant on the issue of transportation to the eastern colonies. Two convict ships were sent directly to the labour-starved Moreton Bay colony in 1849 and 1850. Fortunately for the anti-transportation movement, Lord Grey's Government lost office in 1852 and the new Colonial Secretary, Sir John Pakington, begin to dismantle the transportation system to the eastern colonies. The last convict transport to Van Diemen's Land left England on 27 November 1852, dropping off convicts at Britain's Gibraltar penal colony and completing its final journey to the colonies. The jubilee of Van Diemen's Land's 50th anniversary of settlement was able to celebrate the formal end of transportation on 10 August 1853 and the colony's rebirth as Tasmania in 1855.

Western Australia was the final Australian destination for convict transportation. Opposition to convicts in the Swan River Colony was negligible following the free colonists' 1846 petition to the British Government to introduce convicts. Convict labour on public works projects provided government infrastructure that the less than 6,000 free settlers (in 1850) seemed powerless to construct. The first convict ship arrived off Fremantle in 1850 and the transports continued to arrive for the next 18 years.

In Britain, there was a final flurry of interest in the revival of Australian convict transportation when committees in both houses of Parliament supported proposals for convict labour in the agricultural settlements of northern Australia. On 17 June 1856 the 'Minutes of Evidence from the Select Committee on Punishment in Lieu of Transportation' (House of Lords) heard evidence for a convict labour force from agriculturalists in the Moreton Bay Colony in the area of Port Curtis and Cape York. Grazier MH Marsh, from Darling Downs, told an ill-informed British committee that Cape York was fine grazing country. '...[I]n fact, I never saw land near the sea so good for sheep-farming as at Cape York...'[10]

True to its original vows, the Anti-Transportation League maintained its struggle until West Australian convict transportation ended. On 23 October 1863, the Statement and Appeals of the Anti-Transportation League of Victoria once again called for the suspension of convict transportation to the Swan River colony:

> We use no language of menace, we rely on your justice, but experience warns us that the necessities of states are apt to warp the judgement of rulers, and our well grounded anxieties on this question, for the safety and happiness of all we hold dear upon this earth, cannot, and will not subside until transportation to any part of Australia be abolished at once and for ever.[11]

The last convict vessel to Western Australia arrived on 9 January 1868. This voyage effectively ended convict transportation to the Australian colonies.

ENDNOTES

1   *Report from the Select Committee of the House of Commons on Transportation*, Sir William
    Molesworth, Chairman of the Committee, Henry Hooper, London, 1838, p.21.
2   *Select Committee on Transportation*, p.43, p.49.
3   *Report of The Select Committee on the Renewal of Transportation*, William Charles Wentworth,
    Chair, Legislative Council of New South Wales, 1847.
4   Hugh Thomas, *The Slave Trade: The History of the Atlantic Slave Trade 1440–1870*,
    Picador, 1997, Appendix 4: Selected Prices of Slaves, p.807.
5   *Sydney Morning Herald*, 30 May 1849, p.6.
6   'Garryowen', *Chronicles of early Melbourne 1835–1852*, Fergusson and Mitchell, Melbourne,
    1888, p.522.
7   *Sydney Morning Herald*, 30 May 1849, p.2.
8   'Garryowen', p.525.
9   'Garryowen', pp.525–526.
10 *Minutes of Evidence from the Select Committee on Punishment in Lieu of Transportation*,
    17 June 1856, p.5.
11 *Statement and Appeals of the Anti-Transportation League of Victoria, Pamphlet*, 1863, State
    Library of New South Wales.

LIST OF ILLUSTRATIONS

ACKNOWLEDGMENTS

With special thanks to the following individuals: Segio Aguilera, Charles Allain, Clare Anderson, Marianne Austen, John Austin, Sue Backhouse, Ronald T Banks, Natalie Beattie, Bud Bendix, Valerie Ben Or, Caroline Berlyn, Henry Black, Jennifer Blakely, Richard Borg, Ph.Boyer, Tracey Bradford, Anne Brake, Cheryl Brandner, James Broadbent, Mel Broe, Ray Brookes, R & S Brooks, Jennifer Broomhead, Rosalyn Burge, Dianne Byrne, Cary Carson, Jenni Carter, Madamoiselle Celestin, Barbara & Norman Choson, Swapnesh Choudhury, Emma Clark, John Cochrane, Lynn Collins, Eleanor Conlin Casella, Glenn Cooke, Terry Croker, Richard Crosland, Brian Crozier, Simon Cuthbert, Linda D'Arcy, Bruce Davidson, Anne Day, Alan Dodge, Paul Donnelly, Jane Downing, Simon Drake, Andrew Dudley, Jo Duke, Edward Duyker, Karl Dyktinski, Elizabeth Ellis, Arthur Evans, Cathy Evans, John Falconer, Fred Farrell, Ralph Ferrett, Geoff Ford, Francois Fradet, Robert French, Daniel Fromowitz, Nola Fulwood, Diane Gardiner, Michael Gebicki, Mary Gill, Nan Godet, Lesley Goldberg, Janda Gooding, Charles Gruchy, Jacky Guindet, Shaun Gurton, Rebecca Haagsma, Doug Hall, Ross Harley, Edward Harris, John Hawkins, Karla Hayward, Jade Herriman, Shirley Hew, Megan Hicks, Sara Hilder, Gerald Hoberman, Grant Hobson, Warren Horton, Bruce Howlett, Janet Howse, Dawn Hugh, Gwyneira Isaac, Greg Jackman, Jolyon Warwick James, Dean Jennings, Audrey C Johnson, Wayne Johnson, Jennifer Jones-O'Neill, Ray Joyce, Sabine Juffinger, Yeo Kai Leng, Brian Kennedy, Patricia Kennedy, Karen Kidby,

Glenda King, Hazel Laird, Teresa Larkin, Kevin Leamon, Josef Lebovic, Michael Lech, Judith Levin, Mary Lewis, Eva Liehne, Richard Lindo, Chris Lloyd, Quentin & Edwina Macarthur Stanham, Campbell MacKnight, Brad Manera, Tony Marshall, Megan Martin, Hamish Maxwell-Stewart, Julie McConaghy, Rod McGee, Richard McMillan, Terence Measham, Sylvia Meek, Jeffrey Mellefont, Vaughan Melzer, Peter Mercer, Stephen Meucke, Zayd Minty, Allan Moffat, Jennie Moloney, Andrew Montana, Fama Mor, Wendy Morrow, Michael Nash, Belinda Nemec, Richard Neville, Adam Newcombe, Kay Nicholls, Jennifer Nuske, Sonia Oliveira, Sue Osmond, Ian Pearce, Annette Pedersen, Philippe Peltier, Graeme Powell, Eve Propper, Roland Reeve, Dianne Reilly, David Robert, Greg Robinson, Agata Rostek, Karen Rudd, Patricia Sabine, Dagmar Schmidmaier, Christopher Shain, Myffanwy Sharp, Azizah Sidek, Ann Sidlo, Peter Sinclair, Beverly Skinner, Paul Sooprayen, Nicos Soulolos, Al Sowdon, Nina Stanton, Fiona Starr, Claude Stefani, Ben Still, Petra Svoboda, Leslie Swift, Jolyn G. Tamura, Chris Tassell, Ashley Taylor, Hilary Thomas, Brian Tomes, Peter Tonkin, Michael Trudgeon, Neridah Tyler, Dell Upton, Carlos Pedros Vairo, Robert Varman, Gina Vergara-Bautista, Lindie Ward, Elizabeth Webby, David Wells, Peter Whyte, Ian Williams, Nat Williams, Graeme Wilson, Jen Winlaw, Elspeth Wishart, John Woods, Anthony Wylde, Robyn Ziebell.

With special thanks to the following institutions and organisations:

Adelaide Gaol, Antart, Archives office of Tasmania, Art Gallery of Western Australia, Bermuda Archives, Bermuda Maritime Museum, British Library, Centre de Documentation Pedagogique/Nlle-Caledonie, Consulado General de Mexico, Consulate of the Republic of Mauritius, Crowd Productions P/L, Department of Fair Trading, Department de la photographie/La documentation Francaise, Department of Transport (Tasmania), Direction de L'enseignement de la Culture/de la Jeunesse et des Sports, Etabilissement Cinematographique et Photographique des Armes, Fisher Library/University of Sydney, Fremantle Prison, Genealogical Society of Australia, Guildhall Library of City of London, Hawaii State Archives, Historical Association of Southern Florida, Image Bank, Jadon Digital, John Oxley Library/State Library of Queensland, Library of Congress, Maritime Museum of Ushuaia, Mauritius Archives, Ministere Culture Direction/des Archives de France, Musee des Arts d'Afrique et d'Oceanie/Musee des Beaux-arts de Chartes, Museum of Sydney, Narryna Heritage Museum, National Archives of Canada, National Gallery of Australia, National Gallery of Victoria, National Archives of Singapore, National Library of Australia, National Memorial Cellular Jail, National Museum of Australian Pottery, National Reference Library/Singapore, National Trust of Australia (Victoria), Newcastle Regional Museum, Norfolk Island Museum, Novosti Photo Library, Old Melbourne Gaol, Online Book Store/Singapore, Oriental & India Office Collections/British Library, Pacific Magazine, Parramatta Heritage Centre, Port Arthur Historic Site, Port Macquarie Historical Society Inc., Powerhouse Museum, Provincial Archives of New Brunswick, Queen Victoria Museum & Art Gallery, Queensland Art Gallery, Queensland Museum, Queensland State Archives, Red Ant Design, Robben Island Museum, 73rd Regiment of Foot, Simon Wiesenthal Center/Museum of Tolerance, State Library of New South Wales, State Library of Tasmania, State Library of Victoria, State Records of NSW, Sydney Harbour Foreshore Authority, Tasmanian Museum & Art Gallery, Tasmanian National Parks & Wildlife Services, The Colonial Williamsburg Foundation, The Library of Virginia, The Library/Parliament House (Victoria), United States Holocaust Memorial Museum, Vancouver Holocaust Education Centre, Yad Vashem.

The following films appear in the exhibition and were used by permission:
Bounty Ceremony Re-Enacts History. Norfolk Island. Movietone Productions, 1956; *Beautiful North Coast.* Australian Gazette. Australasian Films, 1920; *For the Term of His Natural Lif*e. Directed by Norman Dawn. Australasian Films, 1927; *Fortress.* Directed by Stuart Gordon. Village Roadshow, 1992; *Heritage.* Directed by Charles Chauvel. Expeditionary Films, 1935. Courtesy of Susanne Carlsson, Curtis Brown (Australia) Pty Ltd, Sydney; *Historic Port Arthur.* Cinesound Review, 1946; *In the Wake of the Bounty.* Directed by Charles Chauvel, Expeditionary Films, 1933. Courtesy of Susanne Carlsson, Curtis Brown (Australia) Pty Ltd, Sydney; *Kanakas Cutting Cane.* Nambour, Queensland. Directed by Fred C Wills, Lumiere, 1899; *Kingston, Norfolk Island.* Directed by John Kingsford-Smith, National Trust, 1967; *Memory Of Van Diemen's Land.* Fox Movietone, 1932; *The Sentimental Bloke.* Directed by Raymond Longford, Southern Cross Feature Film Company, 1919; *The Story of the Kelly Gang.* Directed by Charles Tait, 1906; *The Tenth Straw.* Directed by Robert G. McAnderson, Pacific Films, 1926.

Footage for these films provided by ScreenSound Australia, Filmworld, and Village Roadshow. Thanks to Simon Drake at ScreenSound Australia for advice and assistance.

The following reports were commissioned by the Historic Houses Trust of New South Wales for the preparation of the convict exhibition:
Julia Ball, 'A Preliminary Survey of Provenanced Convict Material in Western

Australia', 1997; Margaret Betteridge, 'International Convict Sites Image Search', 1997; Kathryn Bird, 'Cinema's Representation of the Convict Experience', 1997; Caressa Crouch, 'Convict Provenanced Furniture in Australia', 1998; Linda Drew-Smith, 'Convict Families', 1997; Beverly Earnshaw, 'Convict Revolts, Rebellions and Mass Escapes', 1997; Beverly Earnshaw, 'Female Factories', 1997; Jennifer Harrison, 'Convict Holdings. Moreton Bay Colony' 1997; Ralph Hawkins, 'Tools Used by Convicts', 1997; Justine Larbalestier, 'Convict Themes and Images in 20th Century Science Fiction', 1997; Patricia MacDonald, 'Convict Art and Artists', 1997; John McPhee, 'Convicts and the Popular Arts in Australia', 1997; Veronica Pardey, 'Crime Hysteria in British Popular Prints', 1997; Jai Patterson, 'Ross Bridge Convict Carving and Casts', 1998; Jai Patterson, 'Survey of Convict-Provenanced Objects in Tasmanian Collections', 1997; Clem Sargent, 'The New South Wales Garrison 1788–1842', 1997; Tom Sear, 'A Research Report on Convict Familial Relations', 1999; Dominic Steele, 'An Historical Assessment of Convict Diet in Sydney 1788–1840', 1997; David Thomas, 'Colonial Legal System 1788–1840', 1997; Adam Villara, 'Aboriginal Police', 1997; Kylie Winkworth, 'Hyde Park Barracks and the Material Culture of Convicts', 1990.